OUR LOCKDOWN COOKBOOK

The
Not in Disney Any More
Crew

There are friends, there is family, and then there are friends that become family.

—*UNKNOWN*

In 2020, the world became a peculiar place: we couldn't leave our homes; we stood on our doorsteps and clapped for those who risked their lives to keep us alive; we wondered why there was no toilet paper in the shops. And then there was a bunch of friends who found a lifeline on Telegram. We checked in on each other through the difficult times, we joked, and we shared recipes, oh boy did we share recipes – from cookbooks, from youtube, from our own heads.

This book is a collection of those recipes and a testament to friendship.

Thanks everyone for being there, for sharing your love and laughter, and for continuing to be there.

Our Lockdown Cookbook Copyright © 2021 by The Not in Disney Any More Crew. All Rights Reserved.

All rights reserved. No part of this book may be reproduced in any form or by any electronic or mechanical means including information storage and retrieval systems, without permission in writing from the author. The only exception is by a reviewer, who may quote short excerpts in a review.

Cover designed **by Natasha Duncan-Drake**

Printed in the United Kingdom

First Printing: Nov 2021
Wittegen Press

ISBN- 9-798-7-5709780-0

CONTENTS

Breakfasts, Snacks & Soups 3
Main Courses & Sides 25
Desserts & Sweet Treats 77
Bakes 91
Bread 143
Cocktails 163
Staples 169
Useful Information 179
Who Submitted Each Recipe & Where It Came From 193
List of Recipes 203
Index of Ingredients 207

As many recipes as possible in this book have versions suitable for vegetarians unless otherwise stated with 'M' at the top of the page.

These recipes have been recreated here as faithfully as possible to the original posts, including measurements and comments, but some have been abridged (OMG Nigella's metaphors!) or common elements separated for repeated use.

If you are looking to use specific ingredients, try the index at the back.

There are also a few helpful hints that folks shared in Useful Information.

OUR LOCKDOWN COOKBOOK

The, Not in Disney Any More, Crew

BREAKFASTS, SNACKS & SOUPS

Starting the day, or catching a light bite, there's something here for everyone.

Hash Browns 5
Peanut Butter Brownie Baked Oatmeal 6
Vietnamese Breakfast Pastry (Banh Pateso) (M) 8
Moroccan Chicken and Lemon Soup (M) 10
Potato Peel Soup 12
Roasted Cauliflower Soup 14
Potato & Cheese Soup 16
Dates Wrapped in Bacon with Marcona Almonds (M) 17
Grilled Cheese and Egg Sandwich 18
Maple Chipotle Cashews 19
Olive and Gruyere Puff Pastry Tartlets 20
Patatas Bravas 21
Welsh Rarebit 22

The, Not in Disney Any More, Crew

Hash Browns

Who doesn't love a good Hash Brown for Breakfast?

Ingredients
- 4 medium floury potatoes, peeled (like Maris Piper or King Edwards)
- 1 medium onion
- 1 egg, beaten
- salt and pepper
- vegetable oil, for frying

Method
- Coarsely grate the potatoes and onion into a clean tea towel and then squeeze out the excess liquid by twisting the towel. Place the mix in a large bowl.
- Add the egg, a good couple of pinches of salt and freshly ground black pepper (you need to salt the mixture well otherwise the hash browns can be quite bland). Mix the ingredients well.
- Heat a good glug of oil in a heavy based frying pan and when the oil is hot (but not smoking), add spoonfuls of the potato mixture into the pan and flatten into patties about 1cm/½in thick. Flip over once browned and crispy – about 2–3 minutes each side.
- Serve hot as a breakfast or supper side dish. Especially good with bacon and eggs.

Peanut Butter Brownie Baked Oatmeal

This Peanut Butter Brownie Baked Oatmeal is an indulgent-yet-healthy breakfast with rich chocolatey goodness and just a hint of sweetness.

Ingredients

- 1.5 cups mashed ripe bananas (about 3 medium bananas)
- 1 large egg
- ¼ cup natural peanut butter
- ¼ cup brown sugar
- 1 tsp vanilla extract
- ½ tsp salt
- 1 tsp baking powder
- ½ tsp cinnamon
- 1/3 cup unsweetened cocoa powder
- 2 cups whole milk
- 3 cups old-fashioned rolled oats
- 2 tbsp natural peanut butter (for topping)

Method

- Preheat the oven to 375°F/190°C.
- Mash the bananas well, then place them in a large mixing bowl along with the egg, peanut butter, brown sugar, vanilla, salt, baking powder, cinnamon, and cocoa powder. Whisk until the mixture is mostly smooth (there may be small pieces of banana).
- Add the milk to the chocolate banana mixture, and then whisk until smooth again. Add the dry rolled oats and then stir until combined.
- Pour the oat mixture into a 2-3 quart casserole dish coated with non-stick spray. Drizzle the remaining 2 Tbsp peanut butter over the oats and drag a knife through to create swirls. If needed, warm the peanut butter slightly to make it runny enough to drizzle over the oats.
- Bake the oats in the preheated oven for 45 minutes. Serve warm, or refrigerate until ready to eat.

Vietnamese Breakfast Pastry (Banh Pateso) (M)

This recipe was tracked down and shared.

Ingredients

- 1 box puff pastry (2 sheets)
- 0.4 lb / 180g ground pork
- ¼ large onion (diced)
- 3 tbsp liver pate
- ½ cup peas and carrots (thaw if frozen)
- 1 tsp vegetable oil
- ½ tsp salt
- ½ tsp sugar
- ½ tbsp oyster sauce
- ½ tsp garlic powder
- ½ tsp black pepper
- Egg Wash
    - 1 teaspoon water
    - 2 small eggs

Method

- Remove frozen sheets from box and let thaw at least 15 minutes at room temperature. The pastry should still be a little frozen so it's easier to work with.
- Preheat oven to 400F/200C degrees.
- Prepare the filling: in a large bowl, combine all filling ingredients and mix through. It is best to wear gloves and mix by hand so all the filling is incorporated.
- Divide the filling to 9 meatballs. Set aside on a plate.
- Grab 2 small bowls. Crack the eggs and separate egg yolks and egg whites. Add 1 tsp water to egg white. Set aside.
- Remove the pastry sheets from the wrapper. Lay flat on a chopping board. Using a paring knife, cut the sheets into 9 equal squares.
- Place the filling into the centre of the puff pastry. Brush the border with some egg whites. Place another layer of pastry on top. Use a fork to press and seal the edges together. Repeat with the remaining pastry.
- Place the pastry squares on a plate, brush with some egg yolk.
- Transfer to a greased baking pan and bake for 15 to 20 minutes, until the top is flaky and golden brown. Serve warm.

Moroccan Chicken and Lemon Soup (M)

An old favourite from an old book.

Ingredients

- 2 tbsp sunflower oil
- 2 tbsp extra virgin olive oil
- 600g chicken legs, jointed and skinned
- 2 small onions (roughly chopped)
- 1 leek (cut into 1 cm slices)
- 2 medium carrots (roughly chopped)
- 3 sticks celery (cut into 1 cm slices)
- 2 large garlic cloves (crushed)
- 2 tbsp honey
- 4 tbsp raisins
- 3-4 tsp hot curry powder
- 1 tsp ground cumin
- ½ tsp allspice
- 1L chicken stock
- 50g long grain rice
- Salt and freshly ground black pepper
- I large unwaxed lemon (thinly sliced)
- Garnish
    - 150ml Greek yoghurt
    - 2 tbsp chopped coriander

Method

- Heat the oils with ¼ tsp salt and brown the chicken pieces lightly on both sides. Remove the chicken.
- In the same covered pan, cook the onion gently until soft.
- Add the leeks, carrots, celery and garlic and cook for 2 minutes.
- Stir in the honey, raisins, curry powder, cumin and allspice and stir over the heat for 1 minute.
- Return chicken pieces to the pan with the rice, lemon slices and stir to coat in the spices.
- Pour over the stock, stirring well, and bring to a boil.
- Cover and simmer gently for 20-25 minutes until the chicken is cooked
- Extract the chicken and remove the meat from the bones, returning to the pan.
- Taste for seasoning and serve with swirl of yoghurt and sprinkle with coriander.

Potato Peel Soup

"In the interest of frugality and using up everything we can, I've added… a Potato Peel Soup (my mum used to make / love a variation of this)."

Ingredients
- 20g butter, or rapeseed or sunflower oil
- 1 large or 2 medium onions, diced
- 1 bay leaf
- About 200g potato peelings (about as much as you'd get from preparing a decent-sized tray of roast potatoes)
- 500ml whole milk
- 500ml chicken stock or vegetable stock
- 2 tbsp finely chopped parsley leaves (optional)
- Salt and freshly ground black pepper
- TO GARNISH
    - Fried sage leaves
    - Crisp-grilled bacon

Method

- Heat the butter or oil in a medium saucepan over a medium-low heat and add the onions, bay leaf and a good pinch of salt. Sauté gently, until the onions are soft but haven't taken on much colour, about 10 minutes.
- Add the potato peelings and give everything a very good stir for a minute.
- Pour in the milk and stock, season well with salt and pepper and bring to the boil. Reduce the heat and simmer gently until the peels are very tender – another 10 minutes or so.
- Remove from the heat and cool slightly, then purée in a food processor, blender or using a stick blender until very smooth.
- Return the soup to the pan and reheat gently. Season well with salt and pepper and stir in the chopped parsley, if using.
- Serve in warmed bowls, topped with fried sage leaves and shards of crisp-grilled bacon, if you like. Finish with a generous grinding of pepper.

Roasted Cauliflower Soup

Great lunch and can also add in broccoli.

Ingredients

- 1 large head cauliflower (about 2 pounds), cut into bite-size florets
- 3 tbsp extra virgin olive oil, divided
- Fine sea salt
- 1 medium red onion, chopped
- 2 cloves garlic, pressed or minced
- 4 cups (32 ounces) vegetable broth
- 2 tbsp unsalted butter
- 1 tbsp fresh lemon juice, or more if needed
- Scant ¼ tsp ground nutmeg
- For garnish: 2 tbsp finely chopped fresh flat-leaf parsley, chives and/or green onions

Method

- Preheat the oven to 425F/220C. Line a large, rimmed baking sheet with parchment paper for easy cleanup.
- On the baking sheet, toss the cauliflower with 2 tablespoons of the olive oil until lightly and evenly coated in oil. Arrange the cauliflower in a single layer and sprinkle lightly with salt. Bake until the cauliflower is tender and caramelized on the edges, 25 to 35 minutes, tossing halfway.
- Once the cauliflower is almost done, in a Dutch oven or soup pot, warm the remaining 1 tablespoon olive oil over medium heat until shimmering. Add the onion and ¼

teaspoon salt. Cook, stirring occasionally, until the onion is softened and turning translucent, 5 to 7 minutes.

- Add the garlic and cook, stirring constantly, until fragrant, about 30 seconds, then add the broth.
- Reserve 4 of the prettiest roasted cauliflower florets for garnish. Then transfer the remaining cauliflower to the pot. Increase the heat to medium-high and bring the mixture to a simmer, then reduce the heat as necessary to maintain a gentle simmer. Cook, stirring occasionally, for 20 minutes, to give the flavours time to meld.
- Once the soup is done cooking, remove the pot from the heat and let it cool for a few minutes. Then, carefully transfer the hot soup to a blender, working in batches if necessary.
- Add the butter and blend until smooth. Add the lemon juice and nutmeg and blend again. Add additional salt, to taste (I usually add another ¼ to ¾ teaspoon, depending on the broth). This soup tastes amazing once it's properly salted! You can also add a little more lemon juice, if it needs more zing. Blend again.
- Top individual bowls of soup with 1 roasted cauliflower floret and a sprinkle of chopped parsley, green onion and/or chives. This soup keeps well in the refrigerator, covered, for about four days, or for several months in the freezer.

Potato & Cheese Soup

Potato is good – potato and cheese is even better!

Ingredients
- 1 onion
- 2-3 potatoes (skin on)
- 75g or 2 ¾ oz red split peas or green split peas (If using red split peas, you can add a pinch of brown sugar for sweetness)
- Oil for frying
- 1 L (1 ¾ pints) Vegetable stock
- 5oz/140g Cheese of choice - recipe calls for gruyere but anything is good
- For Croutons
    - Stale bread cubed
    - Melted butter
    - Garlic
    - Dried herbs

Method
- Fry off the onion in the oil
- Chop up potatoes and add to pot, fry for a minute
- Add red split peas, fry for a minute
- Add stock and simmer until cooked through.
- Make croutons by frying the bread cubes in the melted butter, garlic and herbs.
- Add cheese to the soup a couple of minutes before serving and stir in to melt

Both the soup and the croutons will keep for a couple of days in the fridge. If freezing the soup, freeze before adding the cheese.

Dates Wrapped in Bacon with Marcona Almonds (M)

This recipe was tested during the Spanish Tapas Zoom Call.

Ingredients
- 15 Medjool pitted dates
- 15 Marcona almonds
- 5 slices bacon cut into thirds
- 1 lime cut into wedges

Method
- Preheat the oven to 400 degrees F. Line a sheet tray with silicone baking mat or parchment paper.
- Make an incision on one side of each date and insert an almond. Squeeze the date shut in your hand to secure.
- Wrap each date with a bacon strip and secure with a toothpick.
- Place all the dates on the prepared sheet tray. Roast the dates in the oven until the bacon on top is starting to crisp – 5 to 6 minutes. Turn the dates over and cook for an additional 5 to 6 minutes.
- Serve hot with lime wedges as garnish.

Grilled Cheese and Egg Sandwich

Breakfast, lunch or just a snack, this sounds fantastic!

Ingredients
- 2 slices Bread (of your choice)
- Butter for spreading on the bread
- Cheese (something that melts well)
- 1 Egg
- Spring Onion, or Bacon Bits (optional)

Method

Somewhere I picked up this grilled cheese with egg recipe, where you squish the middle of one of the bread slices with a glass to get a hollow, set the slice to frying, grate some cheese in the hollow & crack in an egg, add cheese over the top, then the other slice of buttered bread. Flipping it is a bit of a pain, but the result... 😄

I have been known to add spring onion and bacon bits.

And occasionally, a little grated cheese in the bottom of the pan before flipping, because it glues itself onto the bread and gives you crunchy cheese base.

Maple Chipotle Cashews

This recipe was tested during the Spanish Tapas Zoom Call.

Ingredients
- 2 cups unsalted roasted cashews
- ¼ cup maple syrup
- 1 tbsp chipotle powder
- 2 pinches salt

Method
- Mix chipotle powder and maple syrup.
- Put cashews in a pan. Add maple syrup chipotle mixture and salt. Cook on medium high heat for several minutes, stirring frequently until liquid dissolves. Spread cashews on parchment paper or aluminium foil to cool.

Olive and Gruyere Puff Pastry Tartlets

This recipe was tested during the Spanish Tapas Zoom Call.

Ingredients
- 2 sheets of puff pastry, thawed in the fridge
- Egg wash- 1 egg with a tiny bit of water mixed in- beat it well
- 1 ½ cups of shredded Gruyere cheese, divided in half
- 1 ½ cups of chopped olives of your choice, divided in half

Method
- Preheat your oven to 400F/200C and line your pan with parchment for easy clean up.
- Combine your chopped olives and gruyere cheese shreds. Set aside.
- On a lightly floured surface, roll out your thawed puff pastry dough a tad and cut the dough into 1 1/2-2 inch pieces- I used a round pizza cutter to make this easier.
- Place the dough pieces on your pans with about an inch or so between them.
- Lightly brush your puff pastry pieces with the egg wash.
- Place a decent amount of the olive and cheese mixture in the centre of each puff pastry piece.
- Bake the tartlets for around 20 minutes, turning the pan a little more than halfway through.

Patatas Bravas

This recipe was tested during the Spanish Tapas Zoom Call.

Ingredients
- 1.5kg potatoes, peeled and cubed
- 2 tbsp olive oil
- salt to taste
- 1 onion, finely chopped
- 2 cloves of garlic, finely chopped
- 1 or 2 tsp of hot chilli powder to taste
- 1 tsp Spanish paprika
- 6 ripe tomatoes, chopped (or 400g tin of tomatoes)
    - about 100ml of water (if using fresh tomatoes)
- 1 tbsp wine, white or red (or wine vinegar)
- salt and ground black pepper to taste

Method
- Preheat oven to 200 C / Gas 6. Parboil the potatoes in lots of water for about 10 minutes. Drain then place in a baking dish; mix through half the olive oil and salt and bake till cooked – about 20-30 mins, but check halfway through baking.
- Meanwhile, make the sauce: fry the onion and garlic in some oil till transparent. Stir in the chilli powder and paprika. Then add the tomatoes and water (or the tin and its juice) and the vinegar or wine. Cook for about 20 minutes or until reduced a bit and it looks rich.
- Blend the sauce in a blender or food processor till smooth. Add salt and pepper to taste.
- Serve the potatoes in a dish with the sauce over it.

Welsh Rarebit

If beer is not your thing, milk with a dash of marmite can be substituted.

Ingredients

- 35g butter
- 35g plain flour
- 150ml beer (a sweeter, malty beer is better, I think)
- 1 heaped teaspoonful of mustard
- 2 teaspoons Worcestershire sauce or soy sauce
- ¼ tsp paprika
- a small bunch of chives (or green onions)
- 100g mature cheddar or other well-flavoured cheese
- 1 egg
- 3 thick slices of bread

Method

- Melt the butter over a gentle heat.
- Add the flour and mix thoroughly together – fry this in the pan for a minute or two to cook the flour.
- Add about 100ml of the beer and whisk over a medium heat until it starts to thicken.
- Add more beer in small amounts until a thick sauce texture is achieved.
- Add the mustard, paprika and Worcestershire/soy sauce, whisk together and set the sauce aside to cool.
- Chop and add the chives.
- When the sauce is cooled to room temperature or just above, grate the cheese and add about 75g of it to the sauce – reserve about 25g of cheese
- Add the egg to the sauce and beat it all together.
- Preheat the oven to 180C
- Place the slices of bread on an ovenproof tray.
- Share out the sauce on top of the bread slices, spreading it near to the edges.
- Sprinkle the remaining grated cheese over the top.
- Place in the oven for 15 minutes, or until the top is browned and bubbling.

The, Not in Disney Any More, Crew

MAIN COURSES & SIDES

Filling and tasty meals.

Broccoli Casserole 26
Chicken or Haloumi Kebabs with Pineapple and Chilli 28
Chicken or Quorn Tikka Kebabs 29
Chicken (or not) Tetrazzini 30
Dillegrout (M) 32
Fridge Raid Pasta 34
Frying Pan Pizza 36
Glamorgan Sausages with Red Onion and Chilli Relish 38
Instant Noodles 40
Jambon au Meursault (M) 42
Lasagne 44
Pumpkin & Goats Cheese Risotto 46
Miso and Honey Roast Aubergine 47
Mushroom Roulade 48
Perfect Honey & Mustard Sauce + ... 50
Roasted Aubergine with Pomegranate Molasses and Feta 51
Slow Cooker Balsamic Chicken 52
Souffle Omelette 54
Teri's Cracker Barrel's Hash Brown Casserole 55
Taco Mince Cheesy Pancakes 56
Tofu & Spam Fritters with Egg Fried Rice (M) 58
Turkey Meatloaf (M) 60
Baked Marrow with Mushroom and Cheese Stuffing 61
Garlic & Parmesan Mash 62
Garlic & Parmesan Mash Waffles 64
Italian Potato and Courgette Bake 66
Oven Egg Bites 67
Korean Steamed Eggs 68
Soft Creamy Egg Bites (Instant Pot/ Pressure cooker) 70
Rosemary & Parmesan Potato Waffles 72
Spanish Garlic Noodles 74

Broccoli Casserole

I don't know why they used chicken stock, a vegetable stock would have been fine. I used mature cheddar rather than Colby Al Jack because I have no idea what cheese that is, and hand wavy halved the amounts of everything. It's a hand wavy kind of recipe that would be easy to adapt for personal taste. Also sure soy sauce would work instead of Worcestershire sauce.

Ingredients

- Ingredients
- 2 slices whole-wheat sandwich bread
- 2 lb broccoli florets
- 3 tbsp butter, divided 1tbsp and 2tbsp
- 2 tbsp extra virgin olive oil
- 2 cups diced onion
- 4 cloves garlic, minced
- ⅓ cup all-purpose flour
- 3 ½ cups low-sodium chicken or vegetable broth
- 6 oz reduced-fat cream cheese
- 2 tsp Worcestershire or soy sauce
- ¾ teaspoon ground pepper
- ½ teaspoon salt
- 2 cups shredded Colby Jack cheese, divided 1.5 cups to 0.5

Method

- Preheat oven to 300F/150C. Coat a 9-by-13-inch baking dish with cooking spray.
- Tear bread into pieces and process in a food processor until coarse crumbs form. Spread the breadcrumbs on a baking sheet and bake until dry and crispy, about 10 minutes.
- Meanwhile, bring 1 to 2 inches of water to a boil in a large pot fitted with a steamer basket. Steam broccoli until just tender, 4 to 6 minutes. Chop coarsely and spread evenly in the prepared baking dish.
- Increase oven temperature to 350F/180C.
- Heat 1 tablespoon butter and the oil in a large saucepan over medium-high heat. Add onion and garlic; cook, stirring frequently, until soft and translucent, 3 to 5 minutes.
- Sprinkle flour over the vegetables and cook for 1 minute.
- While stirring, slowly pour in broth. Cook, stirring occasionally, until thickened, about 3 minutes.
- Stir in cream cheese, Worcestershire or soy, pepper and salt, cook, stirring, until smooth, about 2 minutes.
- Remove from heat and stir in 1 1/2 cups cheese. Pour the cheese sauce over the broccoli.
- Melt the remaining 2 tablespoons butter.
- Combine the melted butter and the breadcrumbs in a medium bowl.
- Spread evenly over the broccoli mixture.
- Top with the remaining 1/2 cup cheese.
- Bake until the cheese is melted and the sauce is bubbling around the edges, 25 to 30 minutes.

Chicken or Haloumi Kebabs with Pineapple and Chilli

A true, throw it together and see supper.

Ingredients & Method
- I have no recipes for this BTW, it is kinda eh I'll eyeball it till it tastes good 😊
- The kebabs are literally chunks of chicken (or haloumi – editor addition for veggies, since it sounds kinda nice), chunk of pineapple, repeat, add chilli flakes, bake.

Chicken or Quorn Tikka Kebabs

A lighter bite.

Ingredients
- 2 tbsp Tikka Seasoning Mix
- 4 large Chicken Breasts cut into chunks (or 280g quorn pieces – editor addition for veggie alternative)
- 3 tbsp 0% Fat Yoghurt
- 1 Lemon - juice of
- 2 drops Red Food Colouring (optional)
- Low Calorie Cooking Spray

Method
- If using chicken, cut the chicken breasts into chunks about the size and thickness of a chicken nugget.
- Place quorn or chicken into a non-reactive bowl
- Add the lemon juice and mix well so all of the pieces are coated: add 2 tbsp of the Tikka Seasoning Mix and mix well. Then add the yogurt (and food colouring if you're using it) and mix well. Cover with clingfilm and place in the fridge for at least 1 hour
- Pre-heat an oven to 200°C
- Thread the chicken/quorn onto the bamboo skewers. Spray the skewers with low calorie cooking spray
- Heat a cast iron griddle pan (or mist a frying pan with Frylight & heat, if you don't have a griddle). When the pan is very hot, add the skewers, and cook on each side until the they colour
- Once coloured on all sides, place the skewers in the oven for 5-10 minutes until the they are cooked through.

Chicken (or not) Tetrazzini

You can leave out the chicken and use vegetable stock to make this vegetarian. This recipe makes oodles.

Ingredients

For the Chicken (or not) Tetrazzini:
- 16 oz thin spaghetti or linguine
- 2 lbs cooked chicken breast cubed or shredded, or one rotisserie chicken – or leave this out and up the mushrooms.
- 8 oz button mushrooms thickly sliced – or go wild and pick your favourite mushrooms
- 1 medium onion finely chopped
- 5 garlic cloves minced
- 1/4 cup unsalted butter

For the Creamy Sauce:
- 1/4 cup unsalted butter
- 1/3 cup all purpose flour
- 2 cups chicken or vegetable broth
- 1 cup cream
- 1 tsp salt or to taste
- 1/4 tsp black pepper freshly ground
- 1/4 cup parsley chopped, plus more to garnish (you can leave this out if, like me, you hate parsley: bleurgh!)
- 2 cups shredded mozzarella cheese
- ¼ cup parmesan cheese shredded (or vegetarian Italian hard cheese)

Method

- Preheat oven to 375F/190C
- Cook the pasta in salted boiling water to al dente then drain, rinse with cold water and set aside.
- Add butter to a large pot or Dutch oven over medium-high heat then saute mushrooms until they start to soften and turn golden.
- Add the onion and cook for about 5 minutes or until translucent while mixing.
- Add garlic and cook an additional minute. Once fragrant and softened, remove from heat and transfer the mixture to a bowl.
- Place pan back on medium-high heat, add 1/4 cup butter and whisk in the flour once melted. Cook for about a minute while whisking to make the roux.
- Whisk in the chicken/vegetable stock, season with salt and pepper then whisk in the milk and finally the cream.
- Once thickened add the mushroom and onion mixture (along with the chicken), parsley, and pasta to the cream sauce then fold together so everything is well distributed.
- As you mix sprinkle in 1 cup of shredded mozzarella and the parmesan cheese.
- Transfer to 9x13 casserole dish, smooth out and top with remaining mozzarella cheese.
- Bake for 30 minutes or until bubbling and golden.

Dillegrout (M)

I made half as much as Max made in the original video, and I altered the recipe to work in my Instant pot, and it can do with something to go with it (I did some Jersey Royal new pots) - but the flavour is lovely, just not quite like anything I've had before.

Ingredients
- 120g blanched almonds
- 710ml Sweet white wine
- 1.5kg chicken, 2/3 to 1/3 white to dark meat
- 50g sugar
- ¼ tsp clove
- ½ tsp mace
- 35g pine nuts
- ½ tsp dried ginger
- 1 tsp salt
- 30ml white wine vinegar
- 1 tsp rose water
- ½ tsp ground ginger

Method

Prepare the Meat
- Cut up the dark meat and pound until nearly pulp
- Par boil the white meat whole for 10 mins and then chop into small pieces

Make Almond Milk
- Soak almonds in cool water for several hours
- Then add to a blender with the wine and blend until smooth
- Set up a cheese cloth or strainer over a bowl and pour the pulp into it – let it drain as much as possible on its own before gently squeezing it to get the rest of the liquid out

Main mix
- Add the almond milk to a pan, put over a high heat, add dark meat and bring to a boil
- Add the sugar, clove, mace, pine nuts, dried ginger and salt, plus the white meat and then let it simmer for approx. 1 hour. Then remove from heat.
- In a small bowl, mix the vinegar, rose water and ginger and then stir into the pot.
- Serve with new potatoes or another side of your choice.

Fridge Raid Pasta

So if this crisis has made me do anything (other than worry), it's think about food waste very hard. I've been meaning to do it for ages, but, we all know how it is, good intentions, but never the time.

I had milk that was about to go out of date...so I made my own cottage cheese, which is really easy to turn into homemade ricotta with a stick blender and a little extra milk. ...

If you don't fancy making your own cheese because you don't have any spare milk, actual ricotta or cream cheese would work just as well. As I mentioned this is about raiding the fridge.

Ingredients

For the cheese
- 1l / 4 1/4 cups/ 34 fl oz milk (mine was semi-skimmed)
- juice of 1 lemon or white vinegar (2-3 tbsp)
- 1/2 tsp salt

For the sauce
- home-made cottage cheese
- 1 tsp crushed garlic
- Italian herb mix to taste
- 1 slice/ 18g smoked cheese (or any cheese you happen to have, just something with a bit of flavour)
- a little oil
- 2-3 tbsp milk
- ham cut into small chunks (other options include chicken, tofu, quorn, veggies etc - whatever may be lurking in the fridge)

Enough pasta for 2 people ~150g

Method

To make the cheese
- Put the milk in a heavy base saucepan and bring to light boil.
- Take off the heat and add in the lemon and the salt – stir well and set aside.
- Wait for 10-20 mins for the curds and whey to separate.
- Strain off the whey from the curds using a sieve.
- Congrats, you've made cottage cheese.

To make the sauce
- Using a stick blender, or a normal blender, blend the cottage cheese with a small amount of the reserved whey, or a little milk until smooth and creamy.
- Cook the pasta as instructed on the packet, drain and leave to sit in cold water.
- Put a kettle on to heat water.
- Put a little oil in a small saucepan and heat gently.
- Add the garlic and fry for about a min until fragrant.
- Add the smoked cheese (or chosen cheese) and stir until it begins to melt.
- Add the homemade cream cheese to the saucepan with a couple of table spoons of milk and combine.
- Grind in the Italian herb mix, add the ham (or sauce carrier of choice) and stir.
- If the sauce is too thick, add a little more milk and heat gently until warmed all the way through.
- Refresh the pasta with the hot water from the kettle and drain again.
- Pour the sauce over the pasta, mix and serve in bowls with a grinding of pepper (optional).

Frying Pan Pizza

Quick and easy, just make sure your toppings are pre-cooked.

Ingredients
- 5: Parts Flour (Strong or 00) (500g)
- 3: Parts Liquid (Water) (300g)
- 1 tsp sugar
- 1 tsp salt
- 7g fast acting yeast
- Extra Virgin Olive Oil
- Semolina (Optional)
- Toppings – tomato sauce, cheese and any toppings you fancy

Method

- In a bowl, put the flour and then the sugar, salt and yeast in separate areas of bowl
- Add the warm water and mix with a butter knife until everything is combined
- Cover and leave in the fridge overnight (no kneading required)
- When ready to use, get out of the fridge and bring together gently with your fingers to form a ball
- Put a frying pan (suitable for hob and oven) on high heat until almost smoking and preheat the grill
- For each pizza, take a large handful of dough
- Scatter semolina (or flour) onto a surface and press out the dough into a thin disc that will fit your pan
- Make sure all toppings are pre-cooked
- Lay the dough into the pan
- While the bottom cooks, put on the tomato sauce, cheese and toppings of your choice and finish with some more cheese
- Drizzle over some olive oil
- Then put under a hot grill for 3-4 minutes until the top edges of the pizza are blistering.
- Serve.

Glamorgan Sausages with Red Onion and Chilli Relish

"So, the glamorgan sausages were very nice, but the relish just made them."

Ingredients

For the sausages
- 25g/1oz butter
- 115g/4oz leeks, trimmed, finely sliced (prepared weight)
- 175g/6oz fresh white breadcrumbs
- 2 tbsp chopped fresh parsley
- 1 tbsp chopped fresh thyme
- 150g/5oz Caerphilly cheese or Welsh cheddar, finely grated
- 2 free-range eggs, separated
- 1 tsp English mustard
- ½ tsp flaked sea salt
- 5 tbsp sunflower oil
- freshly ground black pepper

For the red onion and chilli relish
- 2 tbsp sunflower oil
- 2 medium red onions finely sliced
- 1 red chilli, finely chopped
- 2 garlic cloves, crushed
- 75g/2½oz light brown muscovado sugar
- 5 tbsp white wine vinegar

Method

- For the sausages, melt the butter in a large non-stick frying pan and fry the leek gently for 8-10minutes, or until very soft but not coloured.
- Put 100g/3½oz of the breadcrumbs, the parsley, thyme and cheese in a large mixing bowl and mix until well combined. Beat the egg yolks with the mustard, salt and plenty of freshly ground black pepper in a separate bowl.
- Remove the frying pan from the heat and tip the leeks into the bowl with the breadcrumbs. Add the egg yolks and mix together well. Divide into 8 portions and roll into sausage shapes. Place the sausages onto a tray lined with clingfilm.
- Whisk the egg whites lightly until just frothy. Sprinkle 40g/1½oz breadcrumbs over a large plate. Dip the sausages one at a time into the beaten egg and roll in the breadcrumbs until evenly coated, then place on the baking tray. Chill the sausages in the fridge for 30 minutes.
- Meanwhile, for the relish, heat the oil and fry the onions for 20 mins, or until very. Add chilli and garlic and cook for a further 5 minutes, stirring regularly.
- Sprinkle with the sugar and pour over the vinegar. Bring to a simmer and cook for five further minutes, or until the liquid is well reduced and the relish becomes thick and glossy. Remove from the heat, set aside to cool for a few minutes.
- Heat the oil into a large non-stick frying pan and fry the sausages over a medium heat for 10-12 minutes, turning regularly until golden-brown and crisp.
- Serve with a good spoonful of chilli and onion relish.

Instant Noodles

The spice paste is a challenge!

Ingredients

For the spice paste:
- 3 medium onions, quartered
- 2 bulbs of garlic, peeled
- 100ml vegetable oil
- 125ml balsamic vinegar
- 150ml fish sauce
- 150ml light soy sauce
- 100g brown sugar
- 200g chilli paste

For the noodles:
- 40g noodles (per portion) of your choice (you can also buy instant noodles that don't need boiling)
- Whatever extras you want.

Method

- To make the spice paste, blitz the onions and garlic until pulsed but not a smooth paste.
- Put the oil into a pan on a medium heat. When it's hot, add the onions and garlic and cook for 10–15 minutes, until the onions are brown. Now add the vinegar, fish sauce, soy sauce, brown sugar and chilli paste, and cook until the mixture is a thick paste with no liquid. This should take about 20 minutes on a medium to low heat.
- When the spice paste is cooked and cooled, put it into a jar – it should keep in the fridge for 2 months.
- Now to make the noodles. Put a tablespoon of the spice paste into a 500ml jar, along with your portion of noodles and all the other bits.
- Leave it in the fridge, and when you are ready to eat, pour 300ml of boiling water into the jar and pop the lid on. I like my noodles brothy, but if you like a drier noodle, just add less water. These are great for home but also perfect for taking to work.

Jambon au Meursault (M)

Shamelessly stolen from my old 1984 St Michael (aka M&S) French Bistro Cookery book

Ingredients

- 450g (1lb) cooked ham or gammon, sliced - I cut mine into strips and layer them
- 25g (1 oz) butter
- 25g (1oz) plain flour
- 150ml (¼ pint) milk
- 150ml (¼ pint) dry white wine
- 1 tbsp tomato puree (I usually add just under 2 though)
- Salt
- White Pepper
- 3-5 tablespoons grated Parmesan or similar type cheese

Method

- Preheat the oven to 200C (400F, Gas Mark 8)
- Arrange the ham or gammon slices in an ovenproof dish
- Melt the butter in a pan, add the flour and cook for 1-2 minutes, stirring
- Add the milk and bring to the boil, stirring all the time
- Add the wine and bring to the boil again, still stirring. Cook for 1-2 minutes, then stir in the tomato puree, salt and pepper
- Pour the sauce over the ham and then sprinkle the cheese over the top
- Cook in the over for about 20 minutes until hot and browned on top
- Serve with jacket potatoes and/or a light salad or with rice or with pasta.

Can be made earlier in the day and then popped into the oven when required.

I find the sauce a little on the frugal side so usually add a little more than half a pint of liquid. I've been making this for decades so no longer bother with measuring ingredients. It's a nice way to use up any leftover ham or gammon (or white wine, if there ever is such a thing!)

Lasagne

This is a favourite for the standard list.

Ingredients

- 2 tsp olive oil, plus a little for the dish
- 750g lean beef mince or veggie replacement
- 90g pack prosciutto (optional)
- tomato sauce
- 200ml hot beef stock
- a little grated nutmeg
- 300g pack fresh lasagne sheets
- white sauce
- 125g ball mozzarella, torn into thin strips

Method

- To make the meat sauce, heat 2 tbsp olive oil in a frying pan and cook 750g lean beef mince in two batches for about 10 mins until browned all over.
- Finely chop 4 slices of prosciutto from a 90g pack, then stir through the meat mixture.
- Pour over 800g passata or half our basic tomato sauce recipe and 200ml hot beef stock. Add a little grated nutmeg, then season.
- Bring up to the boil, then simmer for 30 mins until the sauce looks rich.
- Heat oven to 180C/fan/160C/gas 4 and lightly oil an ovenproof dish (about 30 x 20cm).
- Spoon one third of the meat sauce into the dish, then cover with some fresh lasagne sheets from a 300g pack. Drizzle over roughly 130g ready-made or homemade white sauce.
- Repeat until you have 3 layers of pasta. Cover with the remaining 390g white sauce, making sure you can't see any pasta poking through.
- Scatter 125g torn mozzarella over the top.
- Arrange the rest of the prosciutto on top. Bake for 45 mins until the top is bubbling and lightly browned.

Pumpkin & Goats Cheese Risotto

"Amounts handwavy, but I estimate this is what I'd do for a pan which may end up serving me 3 portions."

Ingredients
- Risotto rice (see package instructions 2 or 2,5 portions)
- Pumpkin in chunks (400g or thereabouts)
- Stock of choice (I use vegetable; see risotto package for amount, possibly use more)
- Soft goats cheese that will melt (100g)
- Pine nuts
- Olive oil
- Onion

Method
- Chop up the onion and sautée in the olive oil. (If you don't have an onion or simply forget it's fine.)
- Add the risotto rice to the pan, stir around in the oil until the grains are coated.
- Add pumpkin and stock to pan, mix, and simmer until cooked. Stir occasionally.
- Roast the pine nuts. (hot pan, no oil, stir frequently)
- Stir goats cheese into the risotto and allow to melt. Mix well.
- Serve with pine nuts on top.

Miso and Honey Roast Aubergine

"Yum."

Ingredients
- 2 medium aubergines
- 4 tsp white miso paste
- 2 tsp runny honey
- 1 tbsp Kikkoman Naturally Brewed Soy Sauce
- 1 tsp toasted sesame oil
- Thumb-sized piece root ginger, peeled and grated
- 1 clove garlic, peeled and crushed
- 4 spring onions shredded
- 2 tsp sesame seeds

Method
- Preheat the oven to 180°C.
- Slice the aubergines in half length-ways and score the flesh in a diamond pattern, taking care not to cut through the skin.
- Line a baking sheet with grease-proof paper and lay the aubergines on top, cut sides up.
- Mix the miso, honey, soy sauce, sesame oil, ginger and garlic with 2-3 tablespoons of water to make a smooth paste.
- Brush over the aubergine flesh and roast for 20 minutes until golden brown and soft. Sprinkle with the spring onions and sesame seeds, then serve.

Mushroom Roulade

A variation of sorts on the Souffle Omelette. You can vary this really easily and add things like spinach etc. to either the mushroom mix or the roulade. The exact amount of mushrooms is more of a guess, btw. I just check them in a pan and keep my fingers crossed. I used 3 / 4 of a 300g pack of frozen wild mushrooms with a two handfuls of rehydrated shitake mushrooms the last time I made this. You can also add as much or as little cream as you like.

Ingredients

- 250g - 300g mushrooms (whatever you have to hand - can be dried (but rehydrated), fresh or frozen)
- 3-4 eggs, separated (depends on the size of the tin you're using & the size of the eggs)
- 2 finely chopped shallots (optional)
- 1 or 2 cloves of crushed garlic (to taste)
- Good squeeze of lemon juice
- Pinch of thyme or oregano to taste
- 50 - 75 ml of either dry or sweet white wine (optional / depending on your taste)
- A few dashes of Worcestershire Sauce (or Mushroom Ketchup for a veggie version)
- 100 ml of double cream or creme fraiche
- Finely grated parmesan cheese (or Italian hard cheese or similar for a veggie version)
- A little olive oil and butter
- Salt and pepper

Method

- Preheat the oven to 180C
- Chop the mushrooms up and set aside for the moment
- Whisk the egg yolks with a little salt and pepper until they are thick, pale and creamy
- Whisk the egg whites until they are stiff
- Fold the egg whites into the egg yolk mixture. You can also fold a little grated cheese into this at this stage
- Pour the combined egg mixture onto a greaseproof paper lined swiss roll tin and bake for 7-9 minutes (you want it lightly golden brown on top so it is just cooked through).
- Whilst that is in the oven, fry the mushrooms (and shallots, if you are using them) in the olive oil and butter mix. Add the crushed garlic and herbs once they are underway and then the lemon juice and Worcester sauce / mushroom ketchup. Let the mushrooms cook through, adding wine half-way through. Add the cream towards the end reduce down to a slightly thick.
- Get a large sheet of greaseproof paper and put it on a baking tray. Sprinkle with finely grated parmesan
- Turn the roulade base onto the greaseproof paper and peel off the original piece of greaseproof
- Once you are ready to finish it off, spread the cooked mushroom mixture over the roulade base, making sure to leave an inch or so free at the sides
- Carefully roll the roulade up (you can sprinkle any of the finely grated cheese it doesn't pick up on it as you go along). You want a nice swiss roll type shape at the end. Grate a little more cheese on the top, if needed, and then stick back in the oven to reheat (around 6-8 minutes, longer if you made the roulade base in advance)
- Serve with whatever else you feel like!

Perfect Honey & Mustard Sauce +

Add meat and veggies of your choice.

Ingredients

- 1 Onion
- 1 cup water
- 3 tbsp Dijon or Whole Grain Mustard
- 1 tbsp English Mustard
- 2 tbsp honey
- ½ teaspoon dried rosemary
- Salt and pepper to taste
- 2 tsp corn flour
- Meat or veggies of choice

Method

- Brown off the meat/veggies in the pan with some oil. (In an Instant Pot or similar use the sauté function, on hob use a high heat).
- Finely chop the onion, add to the pan and soften.
- Mix water, mustards, honey, rosemary and salt and pepper in a bowl. Add to the pan and stir together.
- If using an instant pot, seal and allow to cook for 15 mins, then do a 10 min natural release. (If using only veggies, reduce the cooking time accordingly).
- If cooking on the stove, simmer gently for 15-20 mins.
- Mix the corn flour with a tbsp of water and make a slurry.
- Add the slurry to the pan, bring to the boil either on the hob or using a saute function in an Instant Pot etc, and allow to thicken - stirring constantly.
- Serve with rice or mash or side of choice.

Roasted Aubergine with Pomegranate Molasses and Feta

"This is yummy."

Ingredients

- 1 large aubergine, cut into long wedges, about 1 pound
- 2 tbsp extra virgin olive oil
- 1 tsp smoked paprika
- 1 tsp coarse salt
- 2 tbsp pomegranate molasses
- ¼ cup crumbled soft feta
- 1 tbsp chopped fresh mint
- Freshly ground pepper to taste

Method

- Preheat oven to 400°F/200C. Coat a large baking sheet with cooking spray.
- Toss eggplant wedges with oil to coat. Add smoked paprika and salt and toss to coat. Spread out on the prepared baking sheet. Roast, turning the eggplant over with a spatula once, until the eggplant is softened and caramelized on the bottom, 18 to 24 minutes.
- Transfer the eggplant to a large platter. Drizzle with pomegranate molasses. Sprinkle with feta, mint and pepper. Serve immediately or at room temperature.

Slow Cooker Balsamic Chicken

A good recipe for the freezer.

Ingredients

- 8-10 boneless skinless chicken thighs
- 1-2 tablespoons extra virgin olive oil
- 1 16 ounce package frozen white pearl onions
- 8 ounces white button mushrooms quartered
- 5 garlic cloves minced
- 2 stems fresh rosemary
- 1 bay leaf
- ¾ cup balsamic vinegar
- 1 cup chicken stock
- 3 tablespoons tomato paste
- ¼ cup brown sugar
- salt and freshly ground black pepper
- 1 tablespoon butter
- ½ cup pomegranate seeds
- ¼ cup flat leaf parsley leaves torn or chopped

Method

- Season chicken thighs with salt and freshly ground black pepper. Heat olive oil in a large frying pan over medium high heat and brown thighs in batches for about 5 minutes on each side or until golden brown. Remove from the pan and set aside.
- Layer the pearl onions, button mushrooms, garlic, fresh rosemary and bay leaf in the bowl of a 6 quart slow cooker. Add the browned chicken to the slow cooker bowl. Mix the balsamic vinegar, chicken stock, tomato paste and brown sugar in a medium bowl or a 4 cup measuring cup and season with salt and pepper. Pour over the chicken and cook on high for 3 hours, testing for doneness and cook another 15 minutes to a half hour until chicken is no longer pink.
- Transfer the chicken to a serving dish and cover with a lid or foil. Separate the liquid from the vegetables, and add the vegetables to the chicken. Add the liquid to a saucepan and cook over medium heat, at a low boil, for about 5 minutes or until reduced by half. Add the butter and whisk until melted and sauce has thickened.
- Garnish the chicken with pomegranate seeds and parsley and serve immediately with rice, mashed potatoes or other grain and balsamic sauce.

Souffle Omelette

Bored of a standard omelette? Try one with bubbles!

Ingredients
- 2 eggs
- Pinch of salt
- Pinch of pepper
- Oil for frying

Methods
- Preheat the oven to 170C ish
- Crack the eggs into a medium sized bowl and add the salt and pepper.
- Whisk the eggs with a hand mixer for 5-7 mins until light yellow and fluffy.
- Heat a spritz of oil (just enough to coat the pan very lightly) in a frying pan suitable for oven use.
- Turn the heat down to its lowest and add the fluffy egg to the pan. Cook for about 3 min with a lid on or a bowl covering the pan.
- Put into the oven sans lid and cook for 5-7 mins, until the top looks kind of scaly.
- Tip out onto a plate and serve

Teri's Cracker Barrel's Hash Brown Casserole

Recipe by Rhonda

Ingredients

- 2 lbs frozen hash browns
- ½ cup margarine or butter, melted
- 1 (10 1/4 ounce) can cream of chicken soup (or mushroom soup for the veggies)
- 1 pint sour cream
- ½ cup onion, peeled and chopped
- 2 cups cheddar cheese, grated
- 1 tsp salt
- 1 tsp pepper

Method

- Preheat oven to 350°F/180C and spray an 11 x 14 baking dish with cooking spray.
- Mix the above ingredients together, place in prepared pan and bake for 45 minutes or until brown on top.

Taco Mince Cheesy Pancakes

"Not giving exact measurements as I do it on the fly but it should be common sense. Use as much of the taco seasoning as needed according to the back of the packet v the amount of mince used. I'd aim for at least 2 pancakes per person, depending on how big they are."

Ingredients

- 2 tbsp taco seasoning (packet or homemade, see Taco Seasoning recipe)
- Warm water (for the taco seasoning)
- Minced beef or vegetarian equivalent
- A little oil for frying the mince, if it is very lean or vegetarian mince
- Cheese sauce (either make your own, see Cheese Sauce recipe, or use a packet (or two))
- Crepes/pancakes (I find the sweet ones, if buying shop crepes, work better with the mince and taco seasoning or, if making your own pancakes, make them thin)
- Grated cheese (I use cheddar but any hard cheese will work)
- Optional – finely chopped onion or shallot

Method

- Preheat the oven to 180C
- Mix the taco seasoning with warm water
- Heat the oil, if using any, and lightly fry the mince (if using onions or shallots add them a minute or two before adding the mince to get them softened a little)
- Add the taco seasoning and fry until this has mostly reduced down
- Get the pancakes and add the mince, maybe two or three tablespoons per pancake depending on how big they are, then roll them up so they form a tube shape.
- Add the rolled-up pancakes to a non-stick or greased ovenproof dish
- Make the cheese sauce either as you usually would if making it yourself or according to the packet/s, if cheating :-) You need enough sauce to cover the pancakes very well (almost smothering them). If I'm making this for 1-2 people, one packet usually works. If you find it isn't quite enough, add a little more milk and some grated cheese. You don't want the sauce too thick but a nice easily pourable consistency.
- Pour the cheese sauce over the pancakes, making sure they are covered well
- Grate some hard cheese over the top
- Cook in the oven for 15-20 minutes, until the grated cheese has melted nicely
- I serve this with a green salad and tomatoes but it goes well with lots of things and is very easily adaptable for those with more exotic tastes than my very pedestrian ones! It's also not as much of a faff as it sounds and can be frozen or reheated.

Tofu & Spam Fritters with Egg Fried Rice (M)

"I know you're thinking "Spam?!" - but trust me, this is delicious and really easy and it's the tofu that makes it so easy and the spam that makes it delicious. My husband hates tofu, but really loves this."
Makes 4 fritters & enough rice for 2

Ingredients
Fritters
- 1/2 block tofu (I used Cauldron Organic Tofu because that's what Morrisons had)
- 1/3 of 200g can of Spam
- 1/2 cup plain flour (ish)
- 1 egg
- 50g panko breadcrumbs (ish)
- black pepper to season
- oil for frying

Rice
- 1 cup white rice
- 2 egg yolks
- 2 spring onions (green onions/scallions) chopped
- salt and pepper to season

Method
- Cook the rice per instructions on the packet and cool down with cold water.
- Cut 4 slices from the tofu about 1cm deep, then cut these in half. Season with black pepper.
- Place the blocks on kitchen paper.

- Cut 2 slices from the spam and cut each in half to the same size as the tofu.
- Dust one side of a block of tofu in flour and press onto the spam. Do the same on the other side so we have a spam sandwich with the tofu as the bread. Repeat for all 4 fritters. Then leave for a minute or so.
- Beat the egg in a shallow bowl, and put the flour on one plate and the bread crumbs on another: cover the tofu/spam tower in flour; dip in the egg with right hand.
- Drop in the bread crumbs with right hand and use left to pat on the breadcrumbs on all sides, turning with left hand. Using separate hands for wet and dry dipping will prevent our fingers becoming caked as well. Repeat for all fritters and leave to stand for 10 mins or so to set up.
- Preheat the oven to about 120C (~250F)
- Take a frying pan and put in about 1,5 cm of oil - heat until a little piece of bread sizzles.
- Place the fritters in the oil and fry until the breadcrumbs go golden on the bottom. Turn over and repeat. Then turn fritters onto their sides and repeat for each face.
- Pop the fritters in the oven to keep warm.
- Take the cold rice and mix through the egg yolks.
- In a pan, add a tbsp of oil and heat. Add the chopped spring onion and fry for a few moments.
- Add the rice and egg to the pan and stir fry until piping hot. (You can add other things to the rice if you like, like soy sauce or other veggies, but it is really nice as is).
- Serve with the fritters and sweet chilli dipping sauce, or dipping sauce of choice. Would be yummy with some stir fried broccoli on the side too.

Turkey Meatloaf (M)

"This is my turkey meatload recipe except I double the turkey (misread the recipe the first time and now I'm used to it!) and mix one part light mince to two parts dark just cos I like the differences in texture."

Ingredients

- 2 eggs
- 3 tablespoons ketchup
- 2 teaspoons Italian seasoning
- 1 teaspoon salt
- ½ teaspoon pepper
- ½ onion finely chopped
- 8 ounces mushrooms coarsely chopped
- ½ cup old fashioned rolled oats
- ¼ cup chopped fresh Italian parsley
- 1 ½ pounds ground turkey dark meat - breast would be too dry

Method

- Preheat oven to 325°F/160C.
- Set out a standard 9" x 5" loaf pan.
- Add eggs to a large bowl and whisk until lightly beaten. Add next 8 ingredients (ketchup through parsley) and stir to combine. With your hands mix in ground turkey, just until combined. (Don't over-mix or your meatloaf will be tough.) Transfer mixture to loaf pan and press to fill, smoothing the top with a spatula or spoon.
- Bake until the internal temperature reaches 160°F/70C, 1 to 1 ¼ hours. Allow to rest for a few minutes before serving. Slice and serve.

Baked Marrow with Mushroom and Cheese Stuffing

Serves 4 as a side and 2 as a main dish.

Ingredients

- 4 slices of marrow (about 1 inch/2.5 cm thick)
- 200g mushrooms (of your choice)
- 100g panko breadcrumbs, or other breadcrumbs
- 120g gruyere cheese
- 1 tbsp parmesan, or Italian hard cheese for veggies
- 1 tbsp Italian Seasoning

Method

Stuffing

- Chop the mushrooms finely and gently fry in a pan with a little oil
- Meanwhile, grate the gruyere and add into a bowl with the breadcrumbs
- Mix in the parmesan and the italian seasoning
- Once the mushrooms are cooked, mix them in
- Preheat the over to 180C fan (190C)

For each slice of marrow

- Take out the seeds, place into a piece of lightly oiled foil and wrap the foil up the sides
- Put in the stuffing, pressing down firmly to pack tightly
- Cover with the foil and place onto a baking tray
- Place into the oven for 20 minutes
- Uncover and then leave for a further 20 minutes or until the stuffing is golden brown.

Garlic & Parmesan Mash

It will keep in the fridge for up to a week. When making ahead, allow to come up to room temp before popping in the over to heat through.

Ingredients

- 2 kg potatoes
- 8 fat cloves of garlic
- Salt and pepper to taste
- 75g butter
- 50g parmesan or veggie equiv

Optional topping

- 50g Dried breadcrumbs or panko
- 50g butter
- 35g Parmesan or veggie equiv

Method

- Peel and quarter the potatoes.
- Bruise the garlic cloves with the back of a knife and slip them out of their skins.
- Place potatoes and garlic in a large pan.
- Cover with water and add some salt (Nigella adds 2 tsp, but I never use that much salt, so go with your normal level).
- Bring to the boil and cook with a lid on until pots are very tender.
- Drain the potatoes over a bowl – KEEP the liquid.
- Put the butter into the still warm saucepan and allow to melt.
- Add the potatoes, garlic and about ½ cup/ 125ml of the cooking liquid back into the saucepan and mash. Add more cooking liquid as you go if you like your mash softer.
- Stir in the parmesan.
- Butter a 30x25cm (ish) baking dish.
- Fill with the mash.
- If using the topping, combine the breadcrumbs, butter and parmesan with the rubbing method to make a crumble.
- Add the crumble over the top of the mash and bake in the over at 200C/180C Fan for 20 mins.

Garlic & Parmesan Mash Waffles

When you have lots of garlic and parmesan mash, of course you're gonna make waffles with it!

Ingredients

- 200g (1 cup) leftover garlic and parmesan mash
- 2 tbsp (30ml) butter
- 4 tbsp (60ml) full fat milk
- 1 egg
- 2 tbsp corn flour
- ½ tsp baking powder
- Spring onion thinly sliced (optional)
- 1 tbsp Parmesan (optional) - I didn't add more because there was already plenty in the mash.

Method

- Melt the butter in the microwave and allow to stand to cool down.
- Put a fork through the mash to loosen it up.
- Whisk the cooled butter, the milk and the egg together.
- Add the mash bit by bit, beating it in gently.
- Whisk in the corn flour and baking powder (plus spring onion and Parmesan if using) until there are no lumps - don't worry, it is a very thick batter.
- Heat the waffle iron as per manufacturer's instructions.
- Put in the batter and spread out with a heat-proof spatula before closing the waffle iron.
- Cooking until going golden brown and crispy on the outside.
- While the waffles are cooking, fry an egg for supreme deliciousness and serve together - Nigella also recommends bacon for those who like it.
- I suspect this would work being fried off in simple patties too if there is no waffle iron available.

Italian Potato and Courgette Bake

You will need a roasting tray or a casserole that will go on the hob.

Ingredients
- 1.2kg potatoes
- 40g flour
- 1 tsp Italian seasoning
- ½ tsp onion granules
- ¼ tsp mild chilli powder
- 1 courgette
- 50ml extra virgin olive oil and a little more for drizzling

Method
- Pre-heat oven to 190C (fan) and 200C otherwise
- Peel and slice the potatoes and put into a bowl
- Slice the courgette and added to the bowl
- Mix the flour, italian seasoning, chilli powder and onion granules, sprinkle over the potatoes and courgette and coat
- Place the oil into the roasting tray or casserole on the hob, heat the oil until it is sizzling.
- Layer the courgette and potato into the pan to cover the bottom and build up
- When all layers are complete, drizzle over some more olive oil, press down the layers
- Cover with foil or casserole lid and place into the oven for 40 minutes or until the potatoes are soft
- Then uncover and bake for a further 20 minutes or until leathery/crispy on top.
- Pour off any remaining oil from the pot and serve

Oven Egg Bites

This recipe is gluten free and keto friendly and can be vegetarian or for meat eaters, depending on taste. Serves 6

Ingredients
- 5 eggs
- ½ cup of shredded gruyere or swiss cheese
- ¼ cup full fat cottage cheese or cream cheese
- ¼ teaspoon salt
- Couple cracks of fresh black pepper
- 2-3 thick slices of bacon, or your favourite veggie substitute.

Method
- Cook the slices of bacon or veggie sub before making the egg bites.
- Pre-heat oven to 300F/150C and place a baking dish that is filled with 1 inch of water on the bottom rack. This will create a humid environment and help the eggs cook evenly.
- Add the eggs, cheese, cottage cheese, salt, and pepper to a blender and blend on high for 20 seconds until light and frothy.
- Spray a muffin tin with a little non-stick spray and fill the tins almost all the way to the top with the egg mixture.
- Divide the chopped bacon or veggie sub equally among all of the muffin tins and bake in the oven for 30 minutes, or until the centre of the egg bites are just set.
- Remove from oven and let cool for 5 minutes. Enjoy!

Korean Steamed Eggs

This is a silky smooth egg dish that is a delight to eat. I eat it with a spoon straight from the pot. Nommy.

Ingredients

Basic

- 2 eggs
- 1/2 cup stock (I used chicken but a nice veggie stock would work brilliantly, or even just water)
- salt and pepper to taste

Variation

- 2 eggs
- 1/2 cup water
- 1 tsp low sodium soy sauce
- 1/2 tsp toasted sesame oil
- salt and pepper to taste

Method

- Beat the egg and stock together with a fork or a small whisk.
- Add the salt and pepper (or other spices of choice) and beat in.
- Pour through a sieve into a heat proof container suitable for steaming - I used a ceramic Camembert baking pot I have (and a deep individual pie dish this morning). Two smaller ramekins would also work if dividing the recipe for 2 people.
- Add the chopped onion if using at this point.

For the Instant Pot

- Put 1 cup of water in the bottom of the pot.
- Put in the pot of egg mixture on a trivet so it is not in the water.
- Put on the lid and make sure the valve is set to sealing.
- Use the steam option and put it on for 10 mins.
- When the beeper goes off, do a quick pressure release, remove the lid and serve.

For the stove

- Set up a deep pan with water in the bottom with a steam rack or something to keep the pot out of the water at the bottom.
- Cover the pot in cling film and place the pot on the stand in the pan.
- Put on a lid and bring to the boil.
- Steam for 15-20 mins until set.

Soft Creamy Egg Bites (Instant Pot/ Pressure cooker)

These are similar to the oven egg bites, but for Instant Pot
This recipe is gluten free and keto friendly and can be vegetarian or for meat eaters, depending on taste.
Serves 2

Ingredients

- 2 large eggs
- 1/4 cup / 41g cottage cheese or ricotta
- 1/4 cup / 60 ml milk
- 1/3 cup / 40g shredded cheese (I used a slice of smoked cheese and cheddar)
- 45g tinned ham/bacon/sausage/veggies (it's about 1/4 tin of ham)
- salt
- pepper
- herbs of choice (optional) – I didn't the first time, but anything that goes with cheese would be lovely, including green onion

Method

- Add the egg, cottage cheese, milk, shredded cheese and herbs/seasoning to a Pyrex jug (a bowl will do, but a spout for pouring makes it much easier).
- Use a stick blender to blend everything together until smooth (herbs might remain a bits, but don't worry).
- Grease the egg moulds well.
- Place ham/bacon/veggies into the bottom of the moulds.
- Pour egg mixture into each mould to just before the top.
- Place on silicon lid, or top with foil.
- Put 1 cup of water in the bottom of the Instant Pot.
- Put the trivet in the bottom of the pot and put the egg moulds on top of this. (The moulds should not be in contact with the bottom of the pot).
- Put on the lid and make sure the valve is to 'sealing'.
- Use the steam option and set for 8 mins.
- When cooking time is finished, allow to natural pressure release for 8-10 mins.
- Take out of the Instant Pot and turn out onto a plate. Eat as is, or serve with ketchup or sauce of choice.

Rosemary & Parmesan Potato Waffles

These are absolutely delicious with eggs and maple syrup - and yes they are savoury waffles, but the salt and sweet is divine.

Ingredients
- 400g / 2 cups mashed potato (I had left over from the night before, but you could use defrosted frozen mash or make it fresh)
- 4 tbsp (60ml) butter
- 8 tbsp (120ml) milk
- 2 eggs
- 45g/ ~3/8cup finely grated Parmesan (or vegetarian equivalent)
- 4 tbsp cornflour
- 1/2 tsp baking powder
- 1 tsp Dried Rosemary (I like to grind it in a pestle and mortar or spice grinder to make it distribute better and release its flavour)
- salt & pepper to taste

Method

- Melt the butter and leave to stand to cool down.
- Preheat the waffle iron.
- Using a fork or something similar, break up the mash so that it is light pieces, not one lump.
- In a large bowl whisk together the cooled butter, eggs and milk.
- Add in the potato a little at a time, whisking it in each time. I used a flat manual whisk, but you could use an electric hand whisk or a bowl mixer if you prefer.
- Add the Parmesan, cornflour, baking powder, rosemary and salt and pepper and beat until smooth(ish).
- Add about an ice cream scoop of batter to each side of the waffle iron if using a square one (ours is electric and looks like a sandwich maker) - if using a round one go with what you are used to and close. You'll soon know if you used too much because it will squidge out the sides 😁.
- Cook for about 7 mins total or until golden brown - different waffle makers will vary.
- If making lots, pop the cooked ones in a low oven until ready to eat.

Spanish Garlic Noodles

If you can't get the Spanish noodles mentioned (like I couldn't) spaghetti broken into quarters works just as well. Made this as a side for Sunday lunch.

Ingredients

- 600 ml vegetable broth
- ¼ tsp saffron threads
- 45ml Extra Virgin Olive Oil
- 1 bulb of garlic
- 200g uncooked Spanish Noodles
- 1 tsp of sweet smoked paprika
- 45g manchego cheese (grated) (you can use whatever hard cheese you fancy here)
- Parsley (chopped) to garnish

Method

- Pour the broth into a saucepan
- Pinch in the saffron
- Heat on a high heat
- In meantime, put a frying pan on medium heat and add the olive oil
- Take the head of garlic, remove the skins from all the cloves and chop finely, and add into the pan, coating each piece in the oil
- Add the noodles to the pan, and mix continuously for about 4 mins (do not brown)
- Add the paprika to the pan, and add a little salt and black pepper – mix
- Add the vegetable broth into the pan and increase the heat to high – mix every 1-2 minutes
- After 5-6 minutes when there is a little bit of broth left, but not much, put a lid on the pan and reduce to low-medium heat and simmer for 3-4 minutes when all the broth has been absorbed.
- Remove the pan from the heat and mix in the cheese
- Serve (you can garnish with parsley)

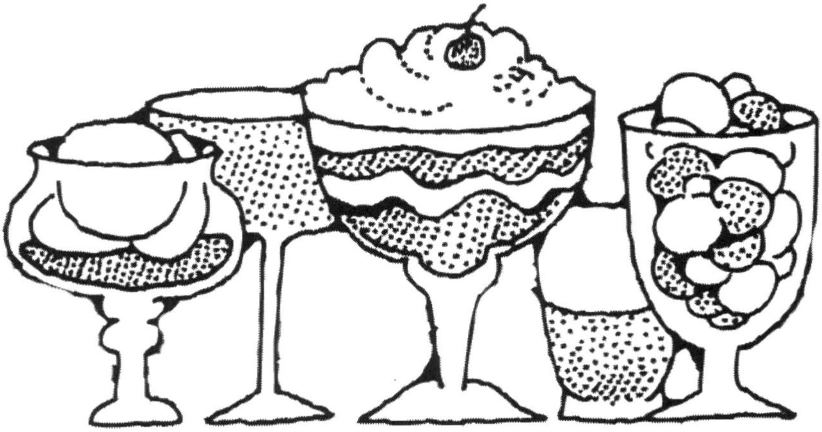

DESSERTS & SWEET TREATS

Stressed spelled backwards is desserts!

Banoffee Pie Using Maple Syrup Caramel 78
Chocolate Date Bites 79
Chocolate Pudding 80
Coconut and Mango Ice Cream 81
Gluten-Free Shortbread 82
Homemade Belgian Waffles 83
Millionaire's Shortbread with Maple Caramel 84
No Bake Strawberry Cheesecake (A Healthier Option) 86
No-Bake Peanut and Ginger Pie 88
Sourdough Pancakes 89

Banoffee Pie Using Maple Syrup Caramel

I love Banoffee, and the maple syrup caramel adds a new dimension.

Ingredients
- Select the No Bake base of your choice (see No Bake Bases in Chapter Staples)
- Caramel Filling (see recipe for Maple Syrup Caramel in Chapter Staples)
- 2 ripe bananas
- 150ml double or whipping cream (I used Elmlea)
- 100g dark chocolate, grated

Method
- Make the base
- While the base is chilling, make the caramel
- Slice your bananas and place over the chilled base
- Pour over the caramel and leave in the fridge to chill and thicken

When ready to serve
- Extract the pie from the pan (unless you're very good, you will probably have to leave the baking parchment on the base) and put on a plate
- Whisk the cream and dollop over the top of caramel
- Scatter the top with grated chocolate

Chocolate Date Bites

These are great for a little sweet bite and a hit of energy.

Ingredients
- 80g oats
- 130g dates (soak in boiling water for 10 mins before using, then drain)
- 100g walnuts
- 10g cocoa powder
- 150g 72% dark chocolate

Method
- Blend oats in a food processor until a fine or semi-fine consistency, depending on taste
- Add dates, walnuts and cocoa powder to the processor and combine until thoroughly mixed and almost a paste.
- Make between 16 and 24 small balls from the mixture, depending on how large you would like the bites.
- Flatten each slightly.
- Melt ¾ of the chocolate in the microwave in 30s sections (usually takes about 3)
- Add in the last ¼ of the chocolate and stir until melted (this should temper the choc).
- Coat the date balls in choc and place on a lined baking sheet.
- Put in the fridge for an hour or so to completely solidify.

Chocolate Pudding

This pudding is fabulous and rich and just yummy!

Ingredients
- 1L of milk (4 cups)
- 250 ml of cream (1 1/20 cup)
- 40 g of cocoa (2/5 cup) (and more for dusting)
- 150 g of dark chocolate
- 70 g potato starch or corn starch (2/3 cup)
- 60 g of sugar (1/4 cup)

Method
- In a bowl whisk the cream and the cocoa together
- In a second bowl, whisk the milk, the starch and the sugar
- Add the chocolate mixture and whisk until incorporated
- Strain into a saucepan, pushing through any clumps
- Add the chocolate and bring the mix to the boil, stirring often
- When it boils, cook for 2 mins
- Put into a lined loaf tin or silicon mould, leave to cool, then cover and freeze for 5-6 hours
- Turn out onto a plate and dust with cocoa to serve

Coconut and Mango Ice Cream

This is fresh and creamy at the same time.

Ingredients

- 1.2 kg / 3–4 cups mango chunks fresh or frozen
- 397 g / 14 oz can coconut milk regular or light
- 107 g / 1/3 cup maple syrup or honey
- 2 tbsp or more any milk or water

Method

- In a blender or food processor, add mango, coconut milk, maple syrup and milk.
- Process until smooth, adding more liquid by tbsp and scraping the walls, if necessary.
- Taste for sweetness now and adjust if necessary. Especially, frozen mango differs.
- Pour into any container and freeze for at least 6 hours or overnight.
- To serve, let thaw on a counter for 30 minutes or 60 minutes for soft serve. It will become softer and creamy.

Gluten-Free Shortbread

This recipe will make slightly more than is needed for the Millionnaire's Shortbread recipe, but that just means cookies as well!

Ingredients
- 1 ⅓ cups white rice flour (7 ½ ounces; 213 grams)
- ½ cup sweet rice flour (2 ½ ounces/ 70 grams)
- ½ cup corn starch (2 ounces/ 56 grams)
- 1 teaspoon salt
- ¼ teaspoon baking powder
- ¼ teaspoon xanthan gum
- 14 tablespoons butter, softened (7 ounces; 198 grams)
- ¾ cup granulated sugar (5 1/4 ounces; 148 grams)
- 1 teaspoon vanilla extract

Method
- Preheat oven to 325°F/160C. Line baking sheet with parchment paper.
- In small bowl, whisk together white rice flour, sweet rice flour, cornstarch, salt, baking powder, xanthan gum.
- In another bowl cream the butter, sugar, and vanilla extract together.
- Add dry ingredients. Mix until a dough forms, but do not overwork.
- Lightly rice flour your countertop. Turn dough out onto counter and shape dough into a disk. Using a rolling pin, roll dough out, until it fits into the 9" loose bottomed baking dish Chill for ten minutes.
- Bake until base is lightly golden brown on the edges and aromatic, about 30 minutes.

Homemade Belgian Waffles

Waffle irons at the ready!
We had 2 recipes shared for sugar waffles, so they gotta be popular!

Ingredients

- 2 ¼ Cups All Purpose Flour
- 1 tbsp Baking Powder
- 3 tbsp Sugar
- ½ tsp Salt
- 1 tsp Cinnamon
- 2 Large Eggs Separated
- ½ Cup Vegetable Oil
- 2 Cups Milk
- 1 tsp Vanilla Extract

Method

- Preheat your waffle iron, spray with non-stick cooking spray and set aside.
- In a large bowl whisk together the flour, baking powder, sugar, salt, and cinnamon.
- In a medium bowl beat the egg whites with a hand mixer until stiff peaks form. Set aside.
- In a separate medium bowl mix together the egg yolks, vegetable oil, milk, and vanilla extract.
- Add the egg yolk mixture to the dry ingredients, mix well.
- Fold in the egg whites.
- Pour the batter onto your hot waffle iron and cook according to manufacturer's directions
- Serve immediately with butter, syrup, powdered sugar or any other favourite toppings.

Millionaire's Shortbread with Maple Caramel

This mixture will fill either a 9" round flan case or a 9" square one. I would suggest one with a removable base, or if not, line it with baking parchment to help with removal from the tin.

Ingredients

Shortbread Base (see alternative Gluten Free Shortbread Recipe if preferred)
- 220g plain flour
- 150g salted butter, cubed from the fridge
- 75g caster sugar

Maple Caramel
- 1/2 cup of maple syrup
- 110g butter
- 300g condensed milk
- Pinch of sea salt if using unsalted butter

Chocolate Topping
- 300g of 72% cocoa dark chocolate

Method

Making the Shortbread
- Pre-heat your oven to 180°C, or 160°C fan
- Sift the flour into a bowl and add the cubed butter.
- Rub the butter between your fingers into the flour, or use a food processor on pulse, or use a pastry blender until you have the consistency of fine breadcrumbs
- Add the sugar and mix in
- Oil your pans
- Put the mixture into the large flan case and press down firmly so the crumbs come together.
- Using a fork, prick the base all over
- Place in the oven for 25 to 30 mins or until shortbread is a light golden colour
- Leave to cool completely

Caramel
- While the base cools, make the caramel (see recipe)
- Pour the mixture over the shortbread and leave at room temperature to set

Making the chocolate topping
- Over a double boiler on the stove, or in the microwave on medium heat at bursts of 30s, melt the chocolate
- Pour over caramel layer and spread out with a spatula
- Leave to cool to room temperature and then place in the fridge to set
- Once everything is set, you can take the shortbread out of the tin and cut into pieces

No Bake Strawberry Cheesecake (A Healthier Option)

Halve the amount of yoghurt and replace with double cream for a more indulgent cheesecake.

Ingredients

- Pick the no bake base of your choice (see No Bake Bases in staples section for more details)

Strawberry Cheesecake Filling

- 454 g (3 cups) fresh or frozen (thawed) strawberries hulled & sliced (plus additional for serving if wanted)
- 118 g cold water
- 2 tbsp / 14 grams unflavoured gelatine or vegetarian equivalent (you may need to alter process accordingly)
- 2 x 8 oz blocks cream cheese room temperature and cut into pieces
- 400 g plain Greek yoghurt 2%+ fat
- 254 g maple syrup or liquid honey
- 1 tsp vanilla extract

Method

Base
- Make the base of your choice, see No Bake Bases in staples section for more details.

Cheesecake Filling
- In a small saucepan, add 1/2 cup cold water and sprinkle gelatine or veg equivalent on top. Set aside and let it bloom while you are making the filling.
- In a food processor, or using a stick blender, add strawberries and process until very smooth and well blended puree forms.
- Place fine mesh strainer over a bowl, pour as much strawberry puree as fits in it and using a spoon push to strain through. You should end up with about 1 cup liquid.
- In a large bowl, add cream cheese and yogurt. Beat until smooth and no lumps, about 5 minutes.
- Add strawberry puree, maple syrup, vanilla and whisk until well combined, pausing and scraping the walls if necessary.
- Place pot with bloomed gel (it will look thick) on low heat. Warm up stirring constantly until gel liquid is clear and thickener has completely dissolved. Remove from heat and let it cool for a few minutes
- Add 1 cup cheesecake filling to it, stir and pour back into a bowl with filling. Beat with a mixer until well combined.
- Pour filling into prepared pan on top of crust. Refrigerate for at least 7 hours or overnight.

No-Bake Peanut and Ginger Pie

Quite a healthy treat. This is enough for a 9 in flan case, or you can also make this with mini cupcake trays, just divide the base and mixture between 22 of them. In the mini versions, they only need 10 mins defrost, so can be really quick treats.

Ingredients
Base
- Make the biscuit no-bake crust with ginger nuts (see No Bake Bases)

Filling
- 250g natural smooth peanut butter
- 3 very ripe medium bananas
- 2 tbsp milk
- 2 tsp vanilla extract
- ¼ tsp salt
- 60g dark chocolate chips

Method
- Make the base

Filling
- While the base is chilling, put everything but the chocolate into a blender or food processor, or use a hand blender
- Blend until smooth
- Spoon onto the chilled base
- Sprinkle over the chocolate chips
- Freeze until solid and keep frozen.
- Take out half an hour before serving to defrost a bit. Each slice comes out like ice cream on a ginger base – yummy!

Sourdough Pancakes

Makes 8 pancakes
This one is for those with lots of sourdough starter.

Ingredients

- 150 grams sourdough starter
- 1 large egg
- 220 grams whole milk
- 1 tbsp butter melted and cooled
- 1 vanilla pod seeds only
- 175 grams flour
- 1 tsp baking powder
- 50 grams sugar

Method

- In a large bowl, whisk the sourdough starter, egg, milk, melted butter and vanilla pod seeds until a thick but fluffy batter has formed.
- Next whisk in the flour, baking soda and sugar making sure that no lumps form.
- Brush your pan with a little oil.
- Pour roughly an eighth of the mix into your pan (see note 1) and cook for 2-3 minutes or until bubbles start to appear on the top side of the pancake and set.
- Flip and then cook for another 2 minutes or until the pancake is cooked through.
- Repeat until all of the mix has been used.
- Serve with your choice of fruit and syrup.

The, Not in Disney Any More, Crew

BAKES

Funnily enough, there are a lot of these! Check out the Going Gluten Free tips in the Useful Information section if you want to make any of these bakes gluten free.

Banana, Chocolate & Rum Loaf 92
The Best Banana Cake I've Ever Had 94
Todd's Wonder Banana Bread 96
Banana, Oatmeal and Choc Chip Cookies 97
Best Ever Chewy Brownies 98
Black Bean Brownies 100
Chocolate Chip Cake 102
Chocolate Chunk Cookies 103
Egg Free Choc Chip Cookies 104
Grantham Gingers 106
Healthier Choc Mayo Cake with Healthy Choc Frosting 108
Honey Nut Cake 110
Italian Water Cake 112
Lamingtons 114
Little Carrot Cakes with Orange and Honey Syrup 116
Magic Custard Cake 118
Mango Crumb Bars 120
Moist Chocolate Cake 122
Peanut Butter and Chocolate Stuffed Cookies 124
Peanut Butter Swirl Brownies 126
Perfect Cheese Scones 128
Plum Upside-Down Yoghurt Cake 130
Pumpkin Zeppole 132
Rosemary and Parmesan Oatmeal Biscuits 134
Sugarfree Oatmeal Cookies 135
The Best Oatmeal Chocolate Chip Cookies 136
Summer Berries Drizzle Cake 137
Sticky Ginger Cake 138
Syrupy Lemon, Olive Oil and Semolina Cakes 140

Banana, Chocolate & Rum Loaf

The rum is 'optional' 😊
"You can do the recipe without any or any combo of rum, maple and choc. Can also use nuts etc but we don't do that cos of allergies at work."

Ingredients

- 85g butter
- 170 caster sugar
- 3 bananas as ripe as possible
- 3 tbsp Rum
- 3 tbsp Maple syrup
- 100g chocolate either all one or diff types
- 2 large eggs
- 225g self-raising flour
- ¼ tsp bicarbonate of soda

Method

- Preheat oven to 160C
- Cream butter with caster sugar. Keep going till you get bored then carry on for a bit.
- Mush 3 bananas (can be two if big), add to mix
- Chop 100g of choc (whatever combo / type you want) add it in,
- Add the rum and maple syrup (just don't add the rum if you don't want to) and 2 large eggs
- Stir all that.
- Add in self-raising flour and bi carb, fold in, make sure not missing any
- Put greaseproof paper into a loaf tin, pour the mixture in (it will be quite 'liquidy' but that's fine)
- Pop into oven for 40 mins then check with a knife, keep adding a bit of time till done (sometimes its 40 mins sometimes it's over an hour depending on the mixture). Be wary that it may be banana on your knife, use your judgement.
- Remove the loaf from the tin to cool

The Best Banana Cake I've Ever Had

Banana cake with cream cheese frosting. And yes, it is nommy 😊. It is lovely and def not healthy in any way shape or form.

Ingredients
Banana Cake
- 3 large ripe bananas (about 1 and 1/2 cups mashed)
- 3 cups (375g) all-purpose flour (spoon & leveled)
- 1 teaspoon baking powder
- 1 teaspoon baking soda
- 1/2 teaspoon ground cinnamon
- 1/2 teaspoon salt
- 3/4 cup (170g) unsalted butter, softened to room temperature
- 1 cup (200g) granulated sugar
- 1/2 cup (100g) packed light or dark brown sugar
- 3 large eggs, at room temperature
- 2 teaspoons pure vanilla extract
- 1 and 1/2 cups (360ml) buttermilk, at room temperature*

Cream Cheese Frosting
- 8 ounces (224g) full-fat block cream cheese, softened to room temperature
- 1/2 cup (115g) unsalted butter, softened to room temperature
- 3 cups (360g) icing sugar, plus an extra 1/4 cup if needed
- 1 teaspoon pure vanilla extract
- 1/8 teaspoon salt

Method

- Preheat the oven to 350°F (177°C) and grease a 9×13" pan.
- Make the cake: Mash the bananas. I usually just use my mixer for this! Set mashed bananas aside.
- Whisk the flour, baking powder, baking soda, cinnamon, and salt together. Set aside.
- Beat the butter on high speed until smooth and creamy – about 1 minute.
- Add both sugars and beat on high speed for 2 minutes until creamed together.
- Add the eggs and the vanilla. Beat on medium-high speed until combined, then beat in the mashed bananas.
- Mix in the dry ingredients in three additions alternating with the buttermilk and mixing each addition just until incorporated.
- Spread batter into the prepared pan. Bake for 45-50 minutes. The cake is done when a toothpick inserted in the centre comes out clean. If you find the top of the cake is browning too quickly in the oven, loosely cover it.
- Remove the cake from the oven and set on a wire rack. Allow to cool completely.
- Make the frosting: In a large bowl, beat the cream cheese and butter together on high speed until smooth and creamy. Add 3 cups icing sugar, vanilla, and salt. Beat on low speed for 30 seconds, then switch to high speed and beat for 2 minutes. If you want the frosting a little thicker, add the extra 1/4 cup of icing sugar (I add it). Spread the frosting on the cooled cake. Refrigerate for 30 minutes before serving.

Todd's Wonder Banana Bread

By Todd VanderHayden

Ingredients

- 2oz butter
- 4oz brown sugar (muscovado is v nice)
- 6oz honey
- 2 eggs
- 3 ripe bananas, mashed
- 6 oz flour
- 1/2 teaspoon baking soda
- 1/2 teaspoon salt
- 1/2 cup sliced nuts (optional)
- Pinch of nutmeg &/or cinnamon (optional)

Method

- Line a 12 x 4 1/2 x 2 1/2 loaf tin with greaseproof/baking parchment (or butter it)
- Preheat oven to 180°C (160°C fan oven)
- Soften the butter till it spreads easily (putting it on the defrost cycle in the microwave works nicely).
- Mix the butter, sugar and honey and beat for a couple of minutes.
- Add the eggs and thoroughly mix in the bananas.
- Sift together the flour, soda, spice(s) and salt and blend thoroughly into the mixture.
- If wanted, finally fold in the nuts.
- Pour batter into lined (or buttered) loaf

Bake for 1 hour, or until a knife inserted in the centre comes out clean.

Banana, Oatmeal and Choc Chip Cookies

Only 3 ingredients!

Ingredients
- 2 large Bananas
- 1.5 cups / 135g Rolled Oats – I picked up gluten free porridge oats
- 1/3 cup Dark Chocolate Chips (I just used a standard 100g packet of Dr Oetker 70% Extra Dark Chocolate Chunks – which is probably loads too much, but it works 😄 – use vegan chocolate chips if required)

Method
- Preheat oven to 350F/180C/Gas Mark 4
- Mash the bananas in a bowl – a fork is okay for squishing the bananas, but a potato masher is much faster 😄.
- Mix the oats and banana and then cover them and let them sit for 20mins or so, so the oats absorb the banana – gives a moister cookie and better structural integrity.
- Add the chocolate chips and mix.
- Make into cookie sized balls and flatten slightly when going on to the baking tray (they come out as they go in)
- Into the oven – I baked mine on the lower end at 15mins and they are moist and chewy.
- Try not to eat them all at the same time. 😄😄😄

Best Ever Chewy Brownies

"What I did was halve the white sugar and use the other half as light brown sugar and the texture was lovely."

Brownies can be stored in an airtight container at room temperature for up to 3 days.

Ingredients
- 1 1/4 cups (249 grams) granulated sugar (or 50/50 white and light brown sugar)
- 5 tablespoons (71 grams) unsalted butter
- 2 large eggs plus 1 egg yolk, cold
- 1 teaspoon vanilla extract
- 3/4 cup (75 grams) unsweetened cocoa powder
- 1/3 cup vegetable oil
- 1/2 cup (63 grams) all-purpose flour
- 1/8 teaspoon baking soda
- 1 tablespoon cornstarch/flour
- 1/4 teaspoon salt
- 3/4 cup (128 grams) semisweet chocolate chips

Method

- Preheat the oven to 325°F/160C. Line an 8x8-inch pan with parchment paper.
- In a microwave-safe bowl, add the butter and sugar. Microwave for about 1 minute, or until the butter is melted. Whisk in the eggs, egg yolk, and vanilla. Stir in the oil and cocoa powder.
- With a rubber spatula, stir in the flour, baking soda, cornstarch, and salt until combined. Stir in the chocolate chips.
- Spread the brownie batter evenly into the prepared pan. Place in the oven and bake for 30 minutes, or until the brownies are set and a skewer comes out with moist crumbs attached. Do not overcook. Let cool completely before cutting and serving.

Black Bean Brownies

For the gluten intolerant folks – these are gluten free, no substitutions required. No added refined sugar or oil either.

Ingredients

- 400g tin of Black Beans
- 2 large eggs
- 155g unsweetened apple sauce (I looked up 1/2 cup and is said 125g, but I had a small 155g jar and it just about filled my 1/2 cup measure, so that's what I'm going with) - I think next time I will use the over-ripe banana idea though, because it's easier to get.
- 15 small or 10-12 Medjool dates (I used the small ones)
- the original recipe has 2 tbsp brewed coffee, but I threw in a tsp of instant coffee for a similar effect, since I didn't have brewed coffee on hand.
- 1 tsp pure vanilla extract
- 50g cacao or cocoa powder (cacao is better for you, but is not as easy to get)
- 1/2 tsp baking powder
- 1/4 tsp salt
- 100g bag of extra dark chocolate chips (I used Dr Oetker's 72% choc chips) - 50g for inside, 50g for the top (this may not be quite the right amounts, but it made it easy for me 😄).

Method

- Preheat oven to 350 degrees F. Line 8 x 8 square baking dish with unbleached parchment paper and spray with cooking spray.
- In a powerful blender or food processor add ingredients in the following order: eggs, applesauce, black beans, cacao powder, coffee, vanilla, baking soda, salt and dates; then process until smooth.
- Add 1/4 cup chocolate chips and stir to mix.
- Pour batter into baking dish, top with 1/4 cup chocolate chips and bake for 30 minutes.
- Remove from the oven and let brownies cool for 5 minutes. Transfer to a cooling rack and let cool completely before slicing. Cut into 16 squares.
- Refrigerate for up to 5 days or freeze if not eating immediately.

Chocolate Chip Cake

No added refined sugar in this recipe
This cake will keep up to a week in an airtight container and it gets better the second day

Ingredients

- 165g (1 1/3 cups) all purpose flour
- 1tsp baking soda
- 1 tbsp corn starch
- 1/2 tsp salt
- 85g (3/8 cup) unsalted butter
- 140ml (~2/3 cup) maple syrup
- 1 large egg
- 1/2 tbsp vanilla extract
- 100g (1 cup) dark chocolate chips

Method

- Preheat the oven to 160C/325F
- Melt the butter in the microwave or in a pan and allow to cool slightly.
- Line a 4x8" baking pan with baking parchment.
- Add the flour, baking soda, corn starch and salt and mix in a bowl.
- Put the melted butter into a large bowl, add the maple syrup and mix. Then add the egg and vanilla to this mixture and whisk until it is light brown.
- Add the dry ingredients into the wet and combine.
- Stir in the chocolate chips.
- Put the mixture into the lined baking pan. Bake for between 25-30 mins until a toothpick comes out clean.

Chocolate Chunk Cookies

There is always room for chocolate chip cookies! Makes 12

Ingredients
- 70g soft brown sugar
- 70g caster sugar
- 125g butter
- 1 egg
- 1 tsp bicarbonate of soda
- 175g chocolate chunks

Method
- Preheat oven to 190C and line a baking tray
- Cream the butter and sugars together
- Add the beaten egg and mix
- Sieve in the flour and bicarbonate of soda and stir in
- Stir in the choc chunks
- Use a dessert spoon and place mixture on the tray (beware they will spread, so separate a little)
- Bake for 10-12 minutes until golden
- Put on a cooling rack
- Eat!

Egg Free Choc Chip Cookies

"Added peanut butter powder so had to add more liquid too, cooked a bit longer."

Store in an airtight tin for up to 2-3 weeks.

Ingredients
- 125g butter or pure vegetable margarine, softened
- 125g caster sugar
- 1 tsp vanilla essence or extract
- 200g self-raising flour
- 1 tsp baking powder/soda
- 1 tbsp water
- Optional: 2 tbsp cocoa powder (to make it chocolate)
- Optional : milk chocolate chips or milk chocolate cut into chips or 2 oreos

Method

- Preheat the oven to 180°C ,350°F or gas mark 4.
- Cream the butter and sugar together(with a wooden spoon) in a large bowl until light, fluffy and golden.
- Stir everything together (vanilla, flour, baking powder and chocolate chips or oreos, add the water and the Coco powder) to make the yummy dough.
- Sprinkle some flour onto a surface and the dough. Roll out the dough and with cookie cutters cut out the shapes and lay them out onto greased, lined baking sheets. Spacing them well apart.
- Bake for about 12 minutes or until golden brown.

Leave on the baking sheets for 5 minutes, then transfer to a wire rack to cool.

Grantham Gingers

"Makes about 50 biscuits. Be careful if you try to make them bigger than about a cubic inch/1.5" as there is a size at which they collapse in on themselves, and no longer form the archetypal internal cave system. Also, they are incredibly sweet, and the slightly more than a cubic inch chunks work out to a 2 to 3 inch biscuit of gorgeous gingery crunchiness. The hollow middle is a design feature. If there is no hollow middle you forgot the self raising bit of the self raising flour. Or made the biscuits too big to achieve the required structural integrity.

If you use gluten free flour, allow the dough to sit for 30mins, and maybe add a little milk/milk alternative to bind it, as gf flour has a gritty texture unless allowed time & extra liquid."

Ingredients

- 12 oz caster sugar (340g)
- 4 oz butter (114g)
- 1 egg
- 9oz self-raising flour (250g)
- 3 teaspoons ginger (or to taste)

Method

- Heat oven to 130C (fan ovens) or 150C (non-fan), and line a couple of baking trays with baking parchment. *Really. You will regret not doing it later when you are chiselling them off the baking sheet.*
- Beat butter and sugar together until pale and fluffy.
- Mix in egg.
- Add ginger, mix in.
- Add flour, mix in, until it makes a somewhat crumbly dough. (add liquid if needed for GF flour)
- Divide into walnut sized pieces, and place about 4 or 5 cm apart on the lined baking sheet (they spread). The easiest way is to roll some of the dough into a sausage about an inch or so thick and chop off generous one inch chunks, and flatten them slightly.
- Place on parchment lined tray
- Bake for about 35-40 minutes, until pale gold
- Be gentle removing them from the oven, they can and will collapse at this stage if poked. Leave to cool and harden on the trays for 10 minutes and then put on a rack to cool the rest of the way. Try not to eat all of them. Twist them slightly to get them off the parchment. *Because you listened to me about using baking parchment, right. Right?*

The recipe also works with lemon or cinnamon, but traditionally they are ginger. The clue is in the name.

Healthier Choc Mayo Cake with Healthy Choc Frosting

Did you get the fact this is a healthier option? This is a very dark cake.

Ingredients
For the cake
- 1 large egg
- 87g 2/3cup plain/all purpose flour
- 23g/ 1/4cup unsweetened cocoa powder
- 1/3 tsp baking powder
- 2/3 tsp baking soda
- a smidgen of salt
- 50ml honey
- 37ml maple syrup
- 1/2 tsp vanilla
- 73g 1/3 cup mayonnaise (full fat or light)
- 1/2 tsp instant coffee dissolved in just under 1/2 cup of water (or just water if you don't want you cake so dark)
- 50g extra dark chocolate chips

For the frosting
- 50g 1/5 cup cocoa powder
- 60g 1/4 cup Greek yoghurt
- 2-3 tbsp honey

Method

- Preheat the over to 160C/320F
- Butter or spray a 7 inch round cake pan (or equiv) and line the bottom with baking paper.
- Sieve together the flour, cocoa, baking powder, baking soda and salt into a bowl – set aside.
- Using a stand mixer with a paddle or a hand mixer, combine the egg, honey, maple and vanilla in a large bowl on high speed for 4-5 mins until they are light in colour and fluffyish in texture.
- Add the mayo and combine on low speed.
- Use a spatula to make sure nothing is stuck to the sides of the bowl.
- Starting and ending with the dry ingredients, add the flour mixture and mix slowly, then some of the coffee/water, and repeat until all the ingredients are combined.
- Fold in the chocolate chips.
- Pour the mixture into the cake pan and place in the oven. Cook for 25-30 mins until a toothpick comes out clean.
- Leave to completely cool on a cake rack.
- Mix all the ingredients for the frosting in a bowl with a spatula or hand mixer.
- Use a spatula or spoon to spread the frosting on the cake.
- Eat!

Honey Nut Cake

This delicious cake is light and not too sweet—perfect for a hobbit breakfast or mid-afternoon snack. Skip the honey glaze to make it less sweet, or dust the cake with sugar instead for the opposite effect. Whipped cream and raspberries don't hurt, either. (Hobbits love both!)

Ingredients

For the cake:
- 1½ cups flour
- 1 stick and 3 tbsp. unsalted butter, room temperature
- ¼ cup raw sugar
- ¼ cup honey
- 3 eggs
- 1 cup coarsely chopped walnuts
- ½ cup plus 1 tbsp. milk
- 1½ tsp. baking powder
- ½ tsp. baking soda
- pinch of salt
- ½ tbsp. ground cinnamon

For the glaze:
- ¼ cup raw sugar
- 3 tbsp. unsalted butter
- ⅓ cup honey
- ⅓ cup coarsely chopped walnuts, toasted

Method

- Pre-heat the oven to 350F/180C
- Butter and flour the cake pan and set aside.
- In a large bowl, beat butter with sugar until smooth and fluffy, add honey and eggs, one at a time, and keep whisking.
- In a medium bowl, sift together flour, baking powder, baking soda, salt, and cinnamon. Stir into the cake mixture, along with the milk. Whisk until the batter is smooth and then fold in walnuts using a rubber spatula.
- Pour batter into prepared pan. Bake until golden brown on top and the cake tester inserted into centre comes out clean, about 45 minutes.
- Transfer pan to a wire rack and let it cool for about 15 minutes.
- Meanwhile, prepare the glaze: place butter, honey, and sugar in a medium saucepan, cook at low heat until butter is melted, and sugar is dissolved completely, about 5 to 7 minutes.
- Remove cake from pan, and place on a serving plate. Using a spatula, gently spread the glaze on top of the cake and on its sides. Sprinkle walnuts all over and serve.

Italian Water Cake

Not just water (obvs)! A Dairy-free, Egg-free, Magic Cake

Ingredients

- 380 ml water
- 80 ml extra-virgin or vegetable oil
- 1 tsp vanilla extract or paste
- 370 gr all purpose flour
- 2 tsp baking powder
- 240 gr sugar
- 4 tbsp cocoa powder (optional)

Method

- Preheat the oven to 180°C/360°F/Gas Mark 4, and arrange a baking tray onto the middle shelf.
- In a small bowl, mix the olive oil, water and vanilla, then set it aside until needed.
- In a large bowl sift the flour together with the baking powder, and mix well with a whisk. Add in the sugar and cocoa powder and mix well.
- Slowly pour the oil+water mix into the dry ingredients, and gently mix with a whisker until combined and lump-free. You can also add a pinch of sea salt to enhance the sweetness of the cake if you want.
- Spray with baking oil a 7-inch springform cake pan with loose base, although not necessary, I recommend placing a disk of parchment paper over the base. Pour in the cake batter and even the top using a spatula.
- Arrange the cake pan onto the middle rack and bake in the oven for about 45 minutes, then insert a toothpick in the middle of the cake. If it comes out dry, your cake is done, otherwise continue to bake for a further 5 minutes, then check again.
- Take the cake out from the oven and allow to cool completely before removing it from the pan.
- Dust generously with optional confectioner sugar if you like, and serve.

Lamingtons

These are yummy!

Ingredients
Cake
- 200g Caster Sugar
- 4 Eggs
- 1 tsp Vanilla Extract
- 200g Plain Flour
- 1 tsp Baking Powder
- 100g Melted Butter

Chocolate Dip
- 50g Melted Butter
- 160ml Whole Milk
- 45g Cocoa Powder
- 290g Icing Sugar
- A good pinch of Salt

Covering
- Something to coat them in – traditional lamingtons use 250g of desiccated coconut

Method

Cake

- Pre-heat oven to 170C
- Whisk the eggs and sugar and vanilla until light and fluffy
- Sift in the flour and baking powder and fold in
- Add in the melted butter
- Pour into a lined and greased pan and into the oven for 25 mins
- Let it cool down overnight

Chocolate Dip

- To the butter whisk in the milk
- Whisk in the cocoa powder
- Whisk in the icing sugar
- Whisk in the salt

Dipping

- Cut the sponge into equal squares
- Just like egging and breadcrumbing, dip each square into the chocolate sauce
- Toss in the coating
- Put out on a rack to set
- Once all are done, put them in the fridge for ten minutes or so

Little Carrot Cakes with Orange and Honey Syrup

"I'm not a fan of nuts and it's rare to find a carrot cake recipe without them."

Ingredients
- 150ml sunflower oil, plus a little for the tin
- 175g light muscovado sugar
- 200g self-raising flour
- 1 tsp bicarbonate of soda
- 2 tsp mixed spice
- 1 orange, zested and juiced (save the juice for the syrup)
- 2 large eggs
- 50g natural yoghurt
- 200g carrots, about 2 large ones, peeled and grated

For the syrup and icing
- 50ml runny honey, plus extra to drizzle (optional)
- 150g mascarpone
- 100g thick natural yoghurt
- 75g icing sugar, sieved
- edible flowers or extra orange zest, to decorate

Method

- Heat oven to 180C/160C fan/gas 4 and oil a 12-hole muffin tin, or line it with muffin cases.
- In a large mixing bowl, mix the sugar, flour, bicarb, mixed spice and orange zest.
- Whisk together the eggs, oil and yogurt, then stir into the dry ingredients along with the grated carrots.
- Pour the mixture into the prepared tin, or divide between the cases, if using, then bake for 20-22 mins until a skewer inserted into the middle comes out clean.
- While the cakes cook, to make the syrup, heat the honey and orange juice in a pan. Bring to the boil, then simmer for a minute until syrupy.
- Turn the cakes out onto a wire rack and leave them to cool a little.
- Spoon a few tsp over each cake while still warm, then leave to cool completely.
- For the icing, mix the mascarpone, yoghurt, and icing sugar until just combined (if you over-mix, it will become runny). Use a palette or cutlery knife to swirl the icing on top of the cakes, drizzle with a little more honey, if you like, and decorate with edible flowers or orange zest.

Magic Custard Cake

As you cook it settles into three layers - firm base, custard middle and cake-like top

Ingredients

- 125g butter, melted & cooled
- 500ml milk
- 1 tsp vanilla extract or vanilla paste
- 130g icing sugar, sifted
- 4 x 70g eggs, at room temperature
- pinch salt
- 1 tbs caster sugar
- 115g plain flour
- finely grated zest of 1 orange (optional)
- extra icing sugar, for dusting

Method

- Preheat oven to 150C, fan-forced. Butter and line 20cm square cake tin with baking paper.
- Warm the milk and vanilla in a small saucepan on the stove until it is lukewarm. Or microwave on MEDIUM for approx. 3 minutes. Set aside.
- With a stand mixer or handheld mixer, whisk the egg yolks and the icing sugar until light and fluffy. Add the melted butter and stir until well combined.
- Now fold the flour into the batter, and slowly add the lukewarm warm milk. It is a very liquidy batter.
- In the bowl of a stand mixer, beat the egg whites with a pinch of salt until they are foamy, add the caster sugar and beat until thick.
- Gently fold in the egg whites, one third at a time. I found it best to use a whisk for this. The whites will look a little curd-like after mixing them in, just try to mix/fold them to the point where there are no big chunks.
- Pour the batter into the prepared cake tin and bake for between 45 - 60 minutes. (mine took 55 minutes, but it will depend on your oven) If you find the top is browning too quickly, just cover with a piece of baking paper. The cake is cooked when there is a sight 'jiggle' when you gently shake the tin. If it is still quite runny, leave it in for another few minutes.
- Remove the tin from the oven and allow the cake to cool completely.
- I like to trim off the edges, but it's not necessary. Cut the cake into serving portions and dust with icing sugar.

Mango Crumb Bars

"Squishy, feel like some adjustment needed, not sure what. They taste nice though!"

Ingredients
- 2 1/2 cups ripe mangoes (small chunks) 2-3 mangoes
- 3-5 tbsp granulated sugar
- 1/2 tbsp corn starch
- 2 cups flour
- 1/2 tsp baking powder
- 1/4 tsp salt
- 3/4 cup cold unsalted butter
- 2/3 cup brown sugar
- 1 large egg
- 1/2 tsp vanilla extract

Method

- Pre-heat oven to 350 degrees F.
- Cut mangoes into small chunks. In a bowl, combine mango chunks, sugar (use more if mango is not ripened) and corn starch. Mix well and set aside.
- In a large bowl, combine flour, baking powder and salt.
- Cut cold (important: make sure it is cold!) unsalted butter into chunks and add to flour mixture.
- If using a food processor, pulse until small crumbs are formed. If using a pastry cutter, cut butter into flour mixture until small crumbs are formed.
- Mix together wet ingredients – brown sugar, egg and vanilla extract. Then add wet ingredients into buttery dry mixture. Mix well – mixture should be slightly crumbly.
- Bring ~2/3 of crumbly mixture to the bottom of a 8" x 8" baking pan lined with parchment paper. Press mixture onto pan to form a layer of crumb pastry
- Add mango mixture, and spread it out evenly.
- Then sprinkle the top with the rest of the crumbles.
- Bake in the oven for 35-40 minutes.
- Remove from oven and let it cool for 5-10 minutes. Then lift parchment paper and bring pastry out from the pan. Let it cool for another 15-20 minutes.
- Cut into 9 square bars. Serve and enjoy!

Moist Chocolate Cake

"I didn't quite believe the recipe when it said "Moist chocolate cake" but it knew what it was on about. It's structural integrity is a bit lacking."

Ingredients

For batter:
- Sugar 2 cups
- Flour 1 3/4 cups
- Cocoa 3/4 cup
- Baking Soda 1 1/2 tsp
- Baking Powder 1 1/2 tsp
- Salt 1 tsp
- 2 eggs
- Milk 1 cup
- Oil 1/2 cup
- Vanilla Extract 2 tsp
- Boiling Water 1 cup

For icing:
- Butter 1 cup
- Cocoa 1 1/2 cup
- Powdered Sugar 2 cups
- Milk 2/3 cup
- Vanilla Extract 1 tsp

Method

- Preheat oven to 360F / 180C. Grase and flour two 9-in baking pans. Set aside.
- In the large bowl of a standing mixer, stir together flour, sugar, cocoa, baking soda, baking powder and salt.
- Add eggs, milk, vegetable oil and vanilla extract. Beat until smooth about 3 minutes.
- Stir in boiling water. You can use rubber spatula to stir. Batter will be very runny.
- Pour batter evenly between the two pans and bake on middle rack of oven for about 30-35 minutes, until toothpick inserted in centre comes out clean with just a few moist crumbs attached.
- Let it cool about 10 minutes before removing from pans. Then cool completely.
- In the meantime, prepare a chocolate buttercream frosting. Use a standing mixer to beat the butter until fluffy.
- Finally add in cocoa, powdered sugar, milk and vanilla extract. Mix until smooth.
- Cut each cake horizontally.
- Spread evenly 2-3 heaped tbsp buttercream frosting over the first layer of cake, cover with second layer and buttercream frosting and continue that process with remaining layers of cake and buttercream frosting. Spread buttercream frosting evenly with a spatula all over the cake.
- Enjoy!

Peanut Butter and Chocolate Stuffed Cookies

Makes 12 x 100g Cookies or 10 x 125g Cookies, depending on how bug you like your cookies! These are lovely eaten warm from the oven with ice cream. If you don't like peanut butter, change the filling to what you do like and replace the peanut butter chips with more dark choc chips. I found the marzipan and cherry pie filling makes a fantastic alternative.

Ingredients

Stuffing
- 120g Peanut Butter

Cookies

Base
- 190g Cold Unsalted Butter chopped
- 135g Light Brown Sugar
- 135g Caster Sugar

Additions
- 200g Dark Chocolate Chips
- 100g Peanut Butter Chips

Dry Ingredients
- 250g Plain Flour
- 110g Self-Raising Flour
- 60g Cocoa
- 1 tsp Salt
- 1.5 tsp Baking Powder

Wet Ingredients
- 2 Eggs
- 1 tsp Vanilla Extract

Method

- Split stuffing into 10 or 12 balls depending on cookie size and put into the freezer until completely frozen, if the stuffing is sloppy, freeze in ice cube tray
- Cube the butter, ensuring it is cold and mix with a stand or hand mixer to reduce it to irregular chunks
- Add the sugar and mix again, but only for a short time leaving rubble (do not cream)
- Add the remaining additions and short mix to make sure distributed
- Mix the dry ingredients together and then mix in main bowl, ensuring everything is mixed into breadcrumb-like mixture.
- Whisk the eggs and add all the wet ingredients
- Mix until it comes together as a dough, but only just
- Split the dough into 12 100g or 10 125g balls
- Form the dough into balls
- Open up the ball and insert the frozen filling
- If you have a coating, roll cookie in the coating (either just on top or all around)
- Freeze for at least another 2 hours, preferably overnight (you can leave your cookies like this in the freezer in an airtight container and get them out to bake fresh when you want them).
- Pre-heat the oven and the baking tray to 190 Fan
- Place the balls about 3in apart
- Bake for 14 mins for 100g balls or 16 mins for 125g balls Leave 10-15 mins to cool if to be eaten warm to allow the cookies to firm up. Otherwise, leave to cool completely and enjoy cold.

Peanut Butter Swirl Brownies

These smell gorgeous when baking in the oven.

Ingredients

Peanut butter mix
- ¾ cup/180g peanut butter
- 2 tbsp maple syrup
- 2 tbsp coconut oil (oil)
- ½ tsp vanilla
- ¼ tsp salt

Brownie mix
- 6oz/170g dark chocolate
- ½ cup/ 120ml coconut oil
- 3 eggs
- ¼ cup/60g brown sugar
- ¼ cup/60ml maple syrup
- 2 tsp vanilla
- ¾ cup/90g flour
- ½ tsp baking powder
- ¼ tsp salt

Method

- Preheat oven to 325F/170C

Peanut butter mix

- Mix all the ingredients together and set aside.

Brownie

- Take the coconut oil and dark chocolate and melt together.
- Mix in the eggs, brown sugar maple syrup and vanilla.
- Into the wet ingredients, mix in the flour, baking powder and salt.
- Add to lined pan.
- Add peanut mixture in lines.
- Swirl with skewer.
- Bake for 25-30 min.

Perfect Cheese Scones

"I really want to add finely shopped chorizo or something like that, maybe next time."

Ingredients

- 450g plain flour (or if using self-raising flour omit the baking powder)
- 6 tsp baking powder
- 1 tsp salt
- 1 tbsp English mustard powder (optional)
- 100g cold butter
- 250g strong hard cheese like mature red leicester or cheddar
- 2 tbsp finely chopped chives (optional)
- 120ml cold milk
- 120ml cold water
- 1 egg, beaten with a splash of milk

Method

- Heat the oven to 220C.
- Put the flour, baking powder, salt and mustard powder into a large mixing bowl and whisk together until smooth and well combined.
- Grate in the butter, then rub it into the flour with your fingertips until it looks like wet sand.
- Finely grate in 225g cheese, add the chives, and then stir to combine. Mix in the milk and water until the dough just comes away from the edge of the bowl; don't handle it any more than is necessary.
- Tip on to a very lightly floured surface and flatten into a rectangle about 2.5cm high. Cut out with a fluted cutter (about 6cm wide for 12 scones), reshaping as necessary while handling the dough as little as possible.
- Put on a baking tray and brush the egg and milk mixture. Grate the remaining cheese over the top and bake for about 12 minutes until golden.
- Allow to cool slightly on a rack before splitting open.

Plum Upside-Down Yoghurt Cake

"I'd play around with the spices and vanilla next time (more of the latter for me)."

Ingredients
For the plum topping:
- 45 g butter I use salted
- 110 g light brown sugar packed
- ¼ tsp ground cinnamon
- 4-5 medium-size plums red or black,
- 1 tsp milk or cream

For the cake:
- 100 g plain yogurt or Greek yogurt
- 200 g granulated sugar
- 3 large eggs
- 1 tsp vanilla extract
- 2 tsp baking powder
- ½ tsp salt
- 190 g all-purpose flour
- 120 ml neutral-flavoured oil sunflower, grape seed, canola oil, etc.

Method
- Preheat the oven to 350°F (175°C). Spray a 9-inch round cake pan (with at least 2-inch tall sides) with baking spray. Line bottom of the pan with parchment paper and spray parchment paper lightly. Set aside.

For the plum topping:
- Melt the butter in the microwave. Add the brown sugar and cinnamon and stir until well combined.

- Microwave for another 30 seconds then add the milk or cream and stir well. Pour into the prepared cake pan.
- Slice the plums in half and twist to separate. Remove the stone. Slice each half into thin, ⅛-¼-inch slices.
- Working from the centre of the pan in, place the plum wedges (slightly overlapping) in a circular pattern over the brown sugar mixture.

For the cake:
- In a large bowl, combine the yogurt, sugar, eggs and vanilla, stirring until well blended. Add the baking powder and salt. Stir well to combine. Add the all-purpose flour. Stir to combine. It's okay if there are a few lumps. You'll work them out after you add the oil.
- Add the oil and stir well. At first, it may seem to separate, but keep stirring till nice and smooth.
- Pour the batter into prepared pan.
- Bake for 35-40 minutes, until the cake feels springy to the touch in the centre and a toothpick or cake tester inserted into the centre comes out clean. Cover loosely with foil if getting too brown near the end and cake is still not done. The best way to test if a cake is done is to use an instant thermometer. The internal temp should be 205-210°F/105C.
- Cool for 10 minutes in the pan, then invert the pan onto a plate or platter. Give the pan a firm little shake. You should hear the cake drop onto the plate. Slowly and carefully lift the pan off of the cake.
- This part is optional, but I like to do it. Use a pastry brush to brush any extra sauce that's left in the pan (or that drips down the sides of the cake) around the edges of the cake. Serve warm or at room temperature with a dollop of whipped cream, if desired.

Pumpkin Zeppole

Made these Italian style donuts today and they are absolutely delicious. I used philadelphia rather than ricotta because I didn't have any of that and it worked really well. They come out fluffy, but with a slight chew. Also, finally something to use the can of pumpkin sitting in the back of my cupboard.

Ingredients
- 1 1/2 cups all-purpose flour
- 1 1/2 teaspoons baking powder
- 1/2 teaspoon fine salt
- 1/2 teaspoon cinnamon
- 1/8 teaspoon freshly grated nutmeg
- 1 cup (8 ounces) fresh ricotta cheese, well-drained
- 1/2 cup plus 2 tablespoons pumpkin puree (or roasted butternut squash)
- 1/4 cup white sugar
- 2 large eggs
- 1 teaspoon vanilla extract
- Canola oil for frying

Method
- In a bowl, mix the flour, the baking powder the salt, the cinnamon and the nutmeg and whisk everything together Then set aside.
- In another bowl, mix the ricotta, pumpkin, sugar, vanilla and eggs and whisk together until smooth and combined
- Put our wet ingredients into our dry ingredients and mix with a spatula to make a loose dough
- Heat your oil to 375F/190C.
- For each zeppole, take a dessert spoon of batter on one spoon, scrape it off into the oil with another spoon and cook for 2mins, turning halfway through.
- Take out of the oil and put on a rack or kitchen towel to drain. Leave for 10-15 mins to cool and finish drying out.

Rosemary and Parmesan Oatmeal Biscuits

Delicious savories.

Ingredients
- 200g oats
- 60-100g plain flour*
- 1 tsp baking powder
- ¼ tsp salt
- 1 tbsp rosemary
- 20g parmesan or veggie replacement
- 80g melted butter
- 80ml hot water

Method
- Preheat oven to 180C
- Sift 40g of the flour into a bowl, add the oats, baking powder, salt, parmesan, rosemary, and mix.
- Add the melted butter and water to the bowl
- Bring the dough together and mix until it does not stick to your hands (*add additional flour if it is too wet, but wait a little because the oats may soak up some of the water over time)
- Roll out on a floured surface to 0.5cm thick and cut out with a cookie cutter
- Place onto baking parchment on a baking sheet and into the pre-heated oven for 20-25 mins, or until golden brown (can take up to 35 mins)

Sugarfree Oatmeal Cookies

Oatmeal, cinnamon and raisins – what's not to love?

Ingredients
- 75g oatmeal
- 100g self-raising flour
- 1 egg
- 1 ripe banana
- 60g raisins
- 80 ml sunflower oil
- 1 teaspoon cinnamon
- 1 pinch of salt
- Baking paper

Method
- Preheat the oven at 175°C and take out the baking tray.
- Mix all dry ingredients in a bowl: 75g oatmeal, 100g self raising flour, 60g raisins, the cinnamon and the salt. Stir everything well with the fork.
- Mash up the banana in a second bowl. Add the egg and the oil. Whisk until you have a homogenous mass.
- Now add the dry ingredients from the first bowl to the second. Do it little by little, and stir in between. This way you don't get lumps in the batter.
- Place the baking paper on the baking tray. Divide the batter into 6 little heaps and shape these into cookies. Use 2 spoons to do so.
- Bake the cookies for 20 minutes.

The Best Oatmeal Chocolate Chip Cookies

"Might reduce the chocolate and add chopped dried apricots or cherries next time."

Ingredients
- 1 1/2 cups flour (195 grams)
- 1 teaspoon baking soda
- 1 1/2 cups rolled oats (quick cooking oats) (190 grams)
- 1 1/2 - 2 cups semisweet mini chocolate chips (270-360 grams)
- 1 large egg (room temperature)
- 1 cup butter (room temperature) (210 grams)
- 1/2 cup granulated sugar (100 grams)
- 1/2 cup brown sugar (90 grams)

Method
- Pre-heat oven to 400F/200C.
- Line one or two cookie sheets with parchment paper.
- In a medium bowl whisk together the flour, salt, baking soda, oats and chips, set aside.
- In another bowl, beat together the egg, butter and sugars until combined.
- Add the dry ingredients to the creamed mixture and mix. Take two tablespoons of dough and roll into balls, place on the prepared cookie sheet. Gently press down with a fork.
- Bake for approximately 8-10 minutes or until golden brown. Let cool completely before tasting. Enjoy!

Summer Berries Drizzle Cake

"Very similar to Lemon Drizzle but with red berries instead."

Ingredients

- 2 large eggs
- 2 tsp vanilla extract
- 175g fruit, stoned and diced weight
- 140g granulated sugar
- 1-2 tbsp citrus juice - lemon, lime or orange
- 175g very soft butter , plus extra for greasing
- 175g golden caster sugar
- 250g self-raising flour

Method

- Heat oven to 180C/160C fan/gas 4. Grease a 900g/2lb loaf tin and line the base and ends with a long strip of baking parchment.
- Put the butter, caster sugar, flour, eggs and vanilla extract into a large bowl and beat with an electric hand mixer for 5 mins until pale and creamy.
- Spread one-third of the cake mix into the tin, then scatter over 50g of the fruit. Spread another third of the cake mix on top, and scatter 50g fruit. Spread rest of the cake mix over and gently spread with the back of a spoon. Bake for 1 hr, until an inserted skewer comes out clean.
- Poke the cake all over with a skewer. Put remaining 75g fruit into a bowl with the granulated sugar. Stir in 1 tbsp of the citrus juice first with a fork, mashing a little of the fruit as you go. Leave in the tin until the cake is cool and the topping is set and crisp.

Sticky Ginger Cake

"This is my mother's ginger cake recipe and I have loved it most of my life. The recipe is enough to make one huge cake, but my mother recommends making two smaller cakes in loaf tins because otherwise the cake sinks in the middle and it's harder to make sure the middle is done and the outside is not over done."

Ingredients

- 8oz | 230g | 2/3 cup Black Treacle (Molasses)
- 8oz | 230g | 1 cup Soft Spread (you can use butter, but a baking spread makes a lighter cake)
- 8oz | 230g | 1 1/4 cup Dark Brown Sugar
- 1 tbsp Golden Syrup (US peeps, if it's not in the baking section, try the international section - at a push you could use corn syrup)
- 1/2 pt (UK) | 285ml | 1 1/3 cup milk (I used semi skimmed, but the recipe probably originally used whole milk - so just use what you have)
- 1/2 tsp Bicarbonate of Soda (Baking Soda)
- 12oz | 340g | 2 3/4 cup self-raising (rising) flour
- 25g | 4 tbsp ginger (yes that really is table spoons not teaspoons)
- 2 tsp cinnamon
- 1 large egg

Method

- Preheat the oven to 150C | 300F | Gas Mark 2.
- Put the loaf tin liners in the loaf tins.
- Put the treacle, soft spread, brown sugar and syrup into a large saucepan.
- Heat gently until these all melt together, stirring at times to make sure it all mixes.
- Measure out the flour, ginger and cinnamon into a bowl and put aside for later.
- Put the milk and egg into a small saucepan and beat the egg into the milk using a small hand whisk or a fork.
- Add the flour, ginger and cinnamon to the treacle mixture in the saucepan and stir together.
- Stir gently in circles to mix in flour, then beat vigorously until all the lumps are gone.
- Heat the milk/egg mixture gently to blood temperature (easiest way to measure is to stick your little finger in every now and then and when it feels like it isn't cold it's at the right temperature :)).
- Add the bicarb to the milk mixture and stir.
- Add the milk mixture to the treacle mixture and stir together.
- Stir as quickly as you can, but take it easy. There will be bubbles showing as the bicarb activates
- Pour the cake batter into the two loaf tins.
- Put the cakes in the oven and bake for about 1hr (stick a skewer into the middle of the cake to check it is done, if not let it cook a little longer).
- Take out of the oven and allow to cool in the tins until cool enough to handle, then turn out onto a wire cake rack to finish cooling.

Syrupy Lemon, Olive Oil and Semolina Cakes

"Someone put this recipe in a Joe/Nicky fic (come for the ImmortaHusbands, stay for the cake!) and it sounds delicious."

Ingredients

Cakes:
- finely grated zest of 3 large lemons
- 150 ml (scant ⅔ cup) extra virgin olive oil (or sunflower oil)
- 175 g (¾ cup + 2tbsp) caster sugar
- 4 large eggs
- 175 ml (⅔ cup + 1tbsp) milk
- 200 g (1 + ¼ cups) fine semolina
- 75 g (½ cup + 2tbsp) plain flour
- 3 level tsp baking powder

Syrup:
- juice of 3 large lemons
- 200 g (1 cup) sugar
- 2 tbsp honey
- 1 whole lemon , very thinly sliced (optional)

Method

- Preheat the oven to 180C/350F/gas mark 4. Grease about 10 mini brioche moulds or mini loaf tins and dust with flour. Or grease a 20cm square cake tin and line with baking parchment.
- In a large bowl, whisk together the lemon zest, olive oil, caster sugar and eggs until smooth. Mix in the milk and semolina then sift together the flour and baking powder and whisk in until smooth. Divide the mixture between the tins, filling them two-thirds full.
- Bake for about 25 minutes for small cakes, or 50 minutes for one large one, until a skewer inserted into the centre comes out clean.
- While the cakes are baking make the syrup. Put the lemon juice in a measuring jug and add enough water to make it up to 300ml (1 + ¼ cups). Pour the liquid into a saucepan and add the sugar and honey, heat gently until the sugar has dissolved then add the lemon slices if using and bring up to a simmer. Simmer for about 20 minutes until the lemon has softened. If you aren't using the lemon then just simmer the liquid for 5 minutes then remove from the heat.
- When the cakes are baked, place them in their tins on a wire rack; pour a generous amount of the syrup over each cake - I used about 3tbsp per cake; they can take quite a lot. Leave in their tins until they have absorbed the syrup then carefully turn out and place on the wire rack to cool. The small cakes have a tendency to 'dome' quite a lot, so if you want then to sit flat you can trim off the dome. Decorate with the lemon slices before serving.

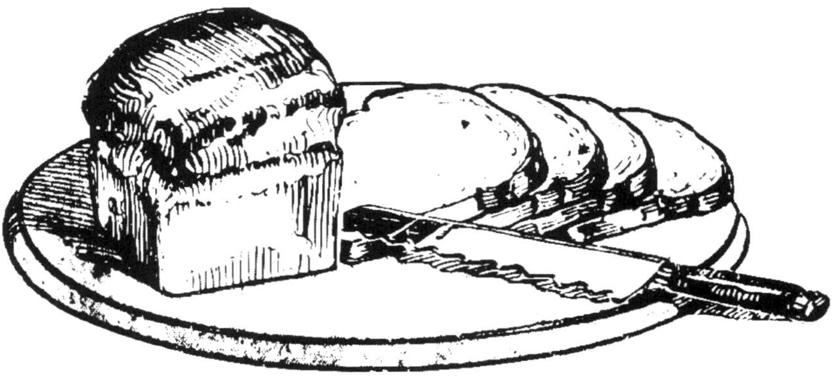

BREAD

Now bread was a popular subject during lockdown, mainly due to a shortage of yeast and flour in the shops and every person and their dog decided to comfort bake!

Crumpets 144
Milk Bread Roll (white) 146
Nadiya's Onion Pretzels 148
Nigella's Old Fashioned Sandwich Loaf 150
No Knead Crusty Chewy Bread 152
Rosemary and Cayenne Pepper Mini Naans 154
Soft Dinner Rolls 156
Sourdough 158
Tangzhong Milk Bread 160

Crumpets

"One thing I have learned - never over fill your crumpet rings, or the holes don't form properly!"

Ingredients

- 175 g strong white bread flour
- 175 g plain white flour
- 14 g fast-action dried yeast
- 1 tsp. caster sugar
- 350 ml warm milk
- 150--200ml tepid water
- 1 tsp. bicarbonate of soda
- 1 tsp. salt
- Sunflower oil for cooking
- At least four 7-8cm metal rings

Method

- Put both flours into a large bowl and mix in the yeast. In a jug, dissolve the sugar in the warm milk, then pour onto the flour mixture. Using a wooden spoon, beat the mixture until you have a smooth batter. This will take three to four minutes and is essential to develop the protein strength in the batter and will ensure the crumpets develop their characteristic holes as they cook.
- Cover the bowl and leave to stand for about an hour. The mixture will rise and then begin to fall. This indicates that the yeast has created its carbon dioxide and is now exhausted. The gluten will now have developed sufficiently to give the crumpets structure and enable them to rise and hold their shape.

- In a jug, mix 150 millilitres of the tepid water with the bicarbonate of soda and salt. Stir this liquid into the batter until evenly combined, then gradually stir in as much of the remaining water as you need to get a thick dropping consistency. Cover the bowl and leave the batter to rest for about 20 minutes. Little holes will appear on the surface and the batter will become a bit sticky.
- Heat a flat griddle or heavy-based frying pan on a medium-low heat. Lightly but thoroughly grease the inside of at least four metal crumpet rings (ideally non-stick). Lightly grease the griddle or pan with oil.
- Put a greased crumpet ring on the griddle. Ladle enough batter into the ring to come just below the rim; it should be about three centimetres deep. The temperature of the pan is important: it is better to cook the crumpet lower and slower than hot and fast. After six to eight minutes, the bottom of the crumpet should be browned and the rest almost cooked through. Top looks almost set and the bubbles that have formed on the surface have burst.
- When the crumpet is ready, the bubbles will stay open rather than fill up with liquid batter. Turn the crumpet over carefully, using two kitchen tools, such as a spatula and a palette knife. Leave the crumpet to cook for another minute or two, then lift it off the griddle onto a wire rack.
- Remove the ring (if it sticks, run a small, sharp knife around the outside of the crumpet to loosen it). Now that you have fine-tuned the time and temperature needed for your batter, you are ready to cook the rest of the crumpets in batches. Serve the crumpets straight away, split or whole, with plenty of butter. Alternatively, leave them to cool on the wire rack and toast them before enjoying with butter.

Milk Bread Roll (white)

Makes 8
Can replace the flour with whatever you like (and add a dash of maple syrup if you want to sweeten the mix)

Ingredients
- 500g strong white bread flour
- 1 tsp salt
- 2 tsp dried yeast
- 30g butter (room temp)
- 100ml milk
- 200ml water
- 1 egg (beaten for egg wash)
- Oil for kneading

Method
- Mix the salt, flour and yeast together in a bowl
- Add the butter in small chunks and rub into the flour
- Measure out the milk into a microwave proof jug and put into the microwave on medium for 30 - 45 sec, depending on the power of your microwave - until the milk is blood warm
- Take water from a not too recently boiled kettle and add enough cold to it that it is also blood warm, add 200ml of it to the milk
- Mix the wet ingredients with the dry until you have a dough that is soft and a little sticky
- Grease your hands and a surface and knead the bread for 20mins until smooth and elastic (you may have to add more oil as the dough gets sticky from time to time)

- Once kneaded, put the dough in a covered, greased bowl and leave to prove in a warm place for 1hr
- After an hour, the dough will have doubled in size
- Put it back on your kneading surface and knock the air out of it
- Divide into 8 equal portions (for my ingredients that was 105g each)
- Roll each portion into a ball and place onto a baking tray covered with baking parchment or a silicone mat about 2cm apart, 3 rolls, 2 rolls, 3 rolls

O O O
O O
O O O

- Cover with a damp tea towel and leave for 40 mins
- Turn on the oven to 200C about 10-15 mins before you are ready to bake and place a baking tray at the bottom
- The rolls should join up slightly once proved.
- Brush the rolls with the beaten egg
- Before putting the rolls in the oven, pour water onto the heated baking tray in the oven to make steam
- Bake the rolls for 15 - 20 mins until golden
- Leave to cool on a wire rack

Nadiya's Onion Pretzels

Makes 12 pretzels.

Ingredients

Pretzel
- 500g bread flour
- 7g fast acting yeast
- 25g caster sugar
- 1 tbsp Onion Granules
- 30g shop bought fried onion flakes
- 2 tsp dried chives
- 50g melted butter
- 300ml warm water

Water for Boiling
- 300ml water
- 3 tbl sp bicarbonate of soda

Topping
- Beaten egg (for brushing)
- Tsp onion granules
- Tsp paprika
- Tsp salt

Method

- Add flour, yeast, caster sugar, onion granules, onion flakes, chives, melted butter and give a little mix
- Add the warm water in a well
- Knead until smooth and stretch 5 mins with mixer, 10 mins by hand
- Leave to prove until doubled in size (about an hour)
- Knock it back and then measure into twelve balls of dough(about 75g)
- Roll each ball into a 30cm long sausage
- Tie a single knot in the dough, then tuck top end under and bottom end over into the knot.
- Put on individual pieces of greased parchment paper and leave to prove for another half an hour
- Preheat oven to 180C
- Bring the water to a boil and add the bicarb
- Take each pretzel on its paper and dunk into the water, dipping the paper below the surface until the pretzel slides off
- 30 sec boil, turning halfway through
- Drain and put onto a baking sheet
- Brush each pretzel with beaten egg
- Mix up the onion granules, paprika and salt
- Sprinkle over pretzels
- Bake at 180C for 12 minutes

Nigella's Old Fashioned Sandwich Loaf

Editor's note – sacrelege, I pruned Nigella's metaphors.

Ingredients

- 500 grams strong white bread flour plus more for dusting
- 2½ teaspoons (7g) or 1 x 7g/¼oz sachet fast-action dried yeast
- 2 teaspoons (8g) caster sugar
- 2 teaspoons (12g) fine sea salt
- 125 millilitres spoilt milk (or sour cream) straight from the fridge
- 150 millilitres cold water
- 100 millilitres hot water from a just-boiled kettle
- 3 x 15ml tablespoons (45g) soft unsalted butter (omit if using sour cream plus more for greasing tin)
- vegetable oil for kneading

You will need a 2lb/900g loaf tin - dimensions vary, but as a guide, mine has internal measurements of 24 x 12 x 8cm / 9.5 x 5 x 3in.

Method

- Mix the flour, yeast, sugar and salt in a large bowl.
- Pour the spoilt milk (or sour cream) into a measuring jug, add the cold water (which will take you to the 275ml / 1½ cups mark) then the boiling water (and I'm presuming you don't need me to say that it should now read 375ml). Stir the soft butter into the jug; it won't melt entirely, but that's fine.
- Pour the wet ingredients into dry ingredients, stirring as you go. Stir until all the flour – apart from a little that's clinging to the sides of the bowl – is absorbed into the dough. Form into a rough ball, cover the bowl with food wrap or a shower cap, and leave for 10 minutes.
- Pour a little oil onto the kitchen counter and spread it with your hand to give a light sheen to an area big enough to knead on. Take the dough out of its bowl and duly knead it for 10 seconds. Form the dough back into a ball, return it to its bowl, cover it again, and leave for 10 minutes. Repeat this process twice, and after the third 10-second knead, form the dough into a ball again, put it back in the bowl, cover, and leave for an hour.
- Line the bottom of a 2lb/900g loaf tin and very lightly grease the sides. Take the risen dough and pat it out on your oiled surface so it's about 2cm thick, with one edge about 4cm shorter than the length of your tin. Starting with this edge, and using both hands, tightly roll the dough into a scroll and place it seam side down in your prepared tin; you may have to press the short sides gently to fit it in. Leave to rise for 1–1½ hours, until top of in
- Pre-heat the oven to 200°C/180°C Fan/400°F. Dust the top of the dough with flour and bake for 45 minutes. Take the bread out of the tin and place it on a wire rack to cool.

No Knead Crusty Chewy Bread

First thing to do when baking this bread? Decide on a timeframe. The dough is stirred together; rests for 10 hours; is put into a crock; rises for 2 hours, and bakes for 45 minutes. So that's just under 13 hours. It's a good weekend bread; stir it together Friday night at about 10 p.m.; scoop it into the crock about 8 a.m. Saturday; bake about 10 a.m., and your bread will be baked, cooled, and ready to slice by noon.

Ingredients

- 5 cups (600g) Unbleached Bread Flour
- 1/4 teaspoon instant yeast
- 2 1/4 teaspoons (14g) salt
- 2 2/3 cups (605g) water, cool
- cornmeal or semolina, for coating the pan

Be sure you have something to bake the bread in, namely a 4- to 4 1/2-quart round, deep covered crock, Dutch oven, or casserole dish. It must be oven-safe (obviously); it really does need a lid, and it has to be deep enough (about 4") to hold the rising dough.

Method

To make the dough:

- Place all of the ingredients in a large mixing bowl. Stir to combine. At first the dough will stick to the spoon and follow it around the bowl. But once all the flour is completely absorbed (after about 10 seconds of vigorous stirring), the dough will become softer and stick to the sides of the bowl. That's it; you're done stirring.
- Cover the bowl and set the dough aside to rest at cool room temperature for 10 to 12 hours. If it's very hot and humid, do your best to find a cooler spot; about 68°F/20C to 70°F/21C is ideal. After its rest, the dough should be very bubbly and will have risen quite a bit.
- Grease your chosen crock with non-stick vegetable oil spray, then sprinkle with cornmeal or semolina, for a nicely crunchy crust. Be sure the crock is well-greased; the last thing you want is for the baked bread to stick.
- Gently stir the dough down, and scoop it into the greased crock. Add the lid and let the dough rest and rise for 1 1/2 to 2 hours at cool room temperature; again, 68°F/20C to 70°F/21C is ideal. Towards the end of the rising time, preheat your oven to 450°F/230C.
- Check the dough before putting it in the oven; it will have risen about 1/2" and show some large bubbles on the surface, though it'll be flat across the top, not domed. Shake the crock very gently; the dough should jiggle a bit.
- To bake the bread: Bake the bread for 45 minutes with the lid on. Remove the lid and bake for an additional 5 to 10 minutes, until the top of the loaf is golden brown with deeper brown blisters (from the bubbles). Remove the crock from the oven, and turn the bread out onto a rack to cool.

Rosemary and Cayenne Pepper Mini Naans

These are rather moreish.

Ingredients

Dry Ingredients
- 7g dried yeast
- 300g strong white bread flour
- 1/2 tsp baking powder
- 1/2 tsp salt
- 1 tbsp rosemary
- 1/4 tsp cayenne pepper
- 1/4 tsp nutmeg

Wet Ingredients
- 2 tsp maple syrup (you can substitute caster sugar in the same quantity if you prefer)
- 2 tbsp vegetable/sunflower oil (plus a little extra for kneading)
- 150ml milk

Method

- Pop the milk in the microwave and warm to blood temperature. This will depend on the microwave, so use 30s bursts at medium power until it's not cold to the touch.
- Add all the Dry Ingredients to a bowl and mix.
- Make a well in centre of the Dry Ingredients and add the milk, oil and maple syrup. Mix everything together to form a soft dough.
- Lightly oil a surface and your hands and then knead the dough on the surface for approximately 10 mins, until the dough is soft, smooth, and elastic. Form into a ball.
- Lightly oil a bowl, put in the dough, cover and leave for 1hr in a warm place, or until the dough has doubled in size.
- Once proved, divide the dough into 12 smaller balls (if you want larger naan, just divide into 6). Place on a baking tray and cover until you need them.
- Heat a non-stick frying pan over a high heat. Then lower the heat to medium. While the pan is heating, roll each ball of dough out to 10cm long and 6cm wide, the dough should be quite thin.
- When the pan is hot, lay as many naans as will fit in your pan (mine did 2 at a time) onto the flat surface and dry fry for 2-3 mins on each side until cooked through. The naan will puff up a little during cooking. You can store the naans in a low oven in a covered dish and separated by baking parchment while finishing them all. Serve warm. Sprinkle over a little oil of your choice (or ghee) to moisten before serving

Soft Dinner Rolls

"I used the mixer to knead the dough for ~5 mins." AUS Measurements.

Ingredients
- 1 tablespoon rapid-rise yeast
- 3 tablespoons white granulated sugar, divided*
- 1/2 cup warm water, (110-115°F)
- 1 cup milk
- 1/4 cup butter, melted
- 1 1/2 teaspoons salt
- 4 cups bread flour, (or all-purpose four), plus about 1/4 cup extra for dusting your work surface
- 2 tablespoons melted butter, for brushing baked rolls

Method
- Mix the yeast, 1 tablespoon of sugar and warm water in a large bowl. Let sit for 7-10 minutes until foamy and frothed.
- While yeast is activating, combine the milk and butter in a 2-cup capacity microwave safe jug. Microwave on high for about 40-50 seconds, or until butter has half melted and milk is luke warm. Stir in remaining sugar and salt. Give it a light mix until the butter completely melts through the milk, and the sugar dissolves. Add to the yeast in the bowl.
- Add in 2 cups of flour, giving it a light mix to combine with a wooden spoon, then add in the remaining 2 cups of flour. Mix until starting to pull away from the walls of the bowl (about 1-2 minutes).

- Turn out on a lightly floured work surface and use the extra 1/4 cup of flour in tablespoon increments to knead until smooth, elastic and slightly sticky
- Transfer dough back into the bowl. Cover with a warm damp towel and proof for 1 hr.
- Scrape dough onto a lightly floured work surface or kitchen bench, knead lightly for about 30-40 seconds if needed to bring the dough together, then divide into 12 pieces.
- Working one by one, lightly flatten each piece of dough in the palm of your hands, then bring up all sides to form a peak on top (like a tent shape), and pinch and seal this peak. Flip it over and arrange rolls, smooth side up into a lightly greased 9x13-inch baking pan or dish (you can line your pan or dish with parchment paper if you wish).
- Preheat oven to 375°F | 190°C (or 350°F | 180°C for fan forced ovens).
- Lightly spray rolls with cooking oil spray, cover with plastic wrap and let rise again until just about doubled in size, (about 30 minutes).
- Bake in a preheated oven for 20-25 minutes, or until rolls are golden browned. (Check them after 18 minutes to make sure they are ok.)
- Lightly brush with a little extra melted butter, and transfer to a cooling rack.

Sourdough

This stuff was all the rage during lockdown!
Editor's note – the original article goes into a lot more detail.

Ingredients
For the leaven:
- 1 tablespoon active sourdough starter
- 75 grams all-purpose flour or bread flour (1/2 cup)
- 75 grams water (1/3 cup)

For the dough:
- 525 grams water (2 1/2 cups), divided
- 1 tablespoon salt
- 700 grams all-purpose flour or bread flour (5 1/2 cups)

Method
- Make sure your sourdough culture is active. If your sourdough has been in the refrigerator, take it out 2 to 3 days before you plan to bake. Feed it daily to make sure it's strong and very active before you make the bread.
- Mix the leaven and let it sit at room temp overnight.
- Dissolve the salt in 50g (about 1/4 cup) of the.
- Add the remaining water to the bowl of leaven and stir.
- Add the flour and stir until it forms a very shaggy dough.
- Cover the bowl and let dough rest for at least 30 minutes or up to 4 hours.
- Pour the dissolved salt over the dough. Work the liquid and salt into the dough by pinching and squeezing.
- Begin folding the dough (2 1/2 hours). To fold the dough, grab the dough at one side, lift it up, and fold it over on top of itself. Fold the dough four times, moving clockwise

from the top of the bowl. Let the dough rest 30 minutes, then repeat. Do this a total of 6 times, every half hour.
- Let the dough rise undisturbed (30 to 60 minutes).
- Use a pastry scraper to divide the dough in half.
- Sprinkle a little flour over each piece of dough for into rounds. Do this a few times to build the surface tension in the dough.
- Rest the dough (20 to 30 minutes).
- Line 2 bread proofing baskets, colanders, or clean mixing bowls with clean kitchen towels. Dust them heavily with flour.
- Transfer to the proofing baskets. Dust the tops and sides of the shaped loaves generously with flour. Place them into the proofing baskets upside down, so the seams from shaping are on top.
- Cover the baskets loosely with plastic wrap, or place them inside clean plastic bags. Let the dough rise (3 to 4 hours, or overnight in the fridge 12-15 hours).
- Heat the oven and two dutch ovens to 500°F/260C.
- Transfer the loaves to the Dutch ovens. Score the top of the loaf.
- Bake the loaves for 20 minutes. Cover and bake for 20 minutes. Reduce the oven temperature to 450°F/230C and bake another 10 minutes. Remove the lids and continue baking 15 to 25 minutes until crust deeply browned.
- When done, lift the loaves out of the pots using a spatula. Transfer them to wire racks to cool completely. Wait until they have cooled to room temperature before slicing.

Tangzhong Milk Bread

"It's a very sticky dough so I have a couple of tips.
- Use a stand mixer or specialised dough mixer if possible. If doing it by hand, oil is going to be your friend.
- Handle the dough with oiled gloves or very oily hands and oiled/non-stick surface."

Ingredients

For the Tangzhong
- 40g Strong White Bread Flour
- 200ml water

For the dough
- 580g/ 4 cups Strong White Bread Flour
- 60g/ ¼ cup sugar
- 12g/ 2 tsp salt
- 10g/ 2.5 tsp dried yeast
- 10g/ 2.5 tsp dried milk powder
- 260g / 1 cup + 2 tbsp milk
- 1 large egg
- 50g/ 1/2 stick unsalted butter (room temp)

For the glaze
- 1 egg yolk
- Milk

Method

The Tangzhong – make in advance (6hrs before)
- Place the flour and water into a shallow pan and heat gently, stirring all the time. Cook until the mixture is a thick paste. Transfer to a container and cover with cling film. Place in the fridge for 6hrs or overnight.
- Take out and allow to come to room temp before using.

The Bread
- Add the flour, sugar, salt, yeast and milk powder to the mixer bowl. Mix to ensure proper distribution.
- Warm the milk in the microwave for 30s until it is luke warm to the touch. Add the egg and whisk together.
- Add the wet ingredients and the tangzhong to the dry and mix on low speed until the dough is beginning to come together. Add the butter to the dough and continue to mix on med until combined. Increase the mixer speed and knead for between 5-10 mins.
- Take the dough out and form into a ball by folding the sides under. Cover in an oiled bowl, allow to rise for 45 mins to 1 hr.
- Divide into six. Roll each into a ball and place under cling film for 15 mins. Lightly oil 2 2lb (9x5") loaf pans.
- Take each ball and roll out into an oval using a non-stick rolling pin. Fold the top point of the oval over the middle and press down with the heel of your hand. Fold the bottom up over the middle and press down with the heel of your hand. Take one of the non-folded edges and press over like the first roll of a swiss roll and press the edge into the main dough with finger tips so it sticks.
- Roll up and seal the edge by pinching it; you have a mini roll the approx width of the loaf pan and 1/3 the length
- Place in one end of the loaf pan. Repeat until there are three rolls in each tin next to each other.
- Cover and allow to rise in a warm spot for 30 mins.
- Pre-heat the over to 180C/355F
- Beat together an egg yolk and a little milk to form the glaze. Brush the tops of the loaves gently with the glaze.
- Bake for 25 mins - they will turn a lovely deep golden brown. Allow to cool on a wire rack.

The, Not in Disney Any More, Crew

COCKTAILS

Boozy things!

Earl Grey Martini 164
Lemon and Ginger Lemonade 165
Mango and Bergamot G&Tea 166
Rosé Sangria 167

Earl Grey Martini

A little touch of posh.

Ingredients
- 50ml gin
- 1 earl grey teabag
- 25ml freshly squeezed lemon juice
- 25ml sugar syrup
- 1 egg white (optional)
- Ice

Method
- Infuse the tea in the gin for 10 minutes at room temperature
- Combine the gin, lemon juice, sugar syrup and egg white into a cocktail shaker
- Dry shake without any ice to emulsify the egg
- Open and add ice; shake again until cold.
- Strain into a chilled cocktail glass

Lemon and Ginger Lemonade

It's got honey in it, so it's good for you!

Ingredients
- 1 lemon and ginger teabag
- 150ml freshly boiled water
- 1tbsp honey
- 150ml cold water
- 50ml high quality gin
- Juice of 2 lemons
- Ice

Method
- Infuse the teabag in the freshly boiled water for 10 minutes
- Add honey and stir until dissolved
- Then add the cold water, gin, lemon juice and ice
- Stir, pour into a tall glass filled with ice and garnish with a slice of lemon.

Mango and Bergamot G&Tea

Who knew gin and tonic could be so versatile?

Ingredients
- 1 Mango and Bergamot teabag
- 100ml 80C water
- 30g sugar
- Gin
- Tonic water
- Ice

Method
- Infuse the tea in the water for 10 minutes
- Stir in the sugar until dissolved then allow to cool
- When ready to drink, just add the G&T, stir and sip in style

Rosé Sangria

This is rather too drinkable.

Ingredients

- 3 nectarines or peaches, stoned and sliced
- 200g strawberries, sliced
- 750ml bottle Spanish rosé wine
- juice 1 orange
- 1 tbsp golden caster sugar
- 50ml orange liqueur (we used Grand Marnier)
- 300ml sparkling water
- small handful mint sprigs

Method

- Put all the ingredients, except the sparkling water and mint, in a large jug and stir to combine.
- Leave in the fridge for about 1 hr or until thoroughly chilled
- Top up with sparkling water and garnish with mint leaves to serve.

The, Not in Disney Any More, Crew

STAPLES

These are recipes you can use over and again as part of many dishes.

Cheese Sauce 170
Maple Syrup Caramel 171
No Bake Base – Biscuit 172
No Bake Base – Nuts & Dark Chocolate.. 173
Perfect Vinaigrette... 174
Taco Seasoning 175
Tikka Seasoning... 176

Cheese Sauce

A great basic to be able to make from scratch.

Ingredients
- 500ml milk
- 4 tbsp plain flour
- 50g butter
- 100g grated, or crumbled cheese, or a mix of cheeses – strong cheddar is great, a dash of parmesan, blue cheese, gouda, Emmental – pick your favourite cheeses
- A dash of ground nutmeg and white pepper to taste (you don't need salt unless your cheese is lacking it)

Method
- Melt the butter in a saucepan and add the flour, keep stirring until combined and cook for a minute or so
- On a low heat, gradually add the milk in 5 or 6 batches, mixing in and ensuring it is fully combined into the roux before adding the next batch – your batches can get bigger as the sauce becomes more liquid
- Add the nutmeg and pepper, and bring the sauce to a simmer
- Simmer until the sauce thickens – don't give up, it takes a little time.
- Remove from heat and stir in the cheese
- Pour over whatever you want.

Maple Syrup Caramel

This stuff is fab, and there's no issue with crystalisation.

Ingredients
- 1/2 cup of maple syrup
- 150g butter
- 1x397g condensed milk
- Pinch of sea salt if using unsalted butter

Equipment
- Thick bottomed saucepan
- Spoon
- Candy or other cooking Thermometer

Method
- Put the maple syrup into a thick bottomed saucepan – this needs to be large to allow the syrup to bubble up
- The syrup should not bubble all the way up, but Just in case, rub a knob of butter around the inside edge of the saucepan, which will turn the bubbles back.
- On a medium heat, bring the maple syrup to the boil and cook until it reaches 225F/110C just below the soft ball stage on a candy thermometer (you may have to tip the syrup to get it to cover the ball of the thermometer)
- Then add the butter and combine
- Finally, add the condensed milk and bring the mixture back up to the boil (slowly so as not to burn it), keep stirring
- Remove from the heat

No Bake Base – Biscuit

This can be used with any no-bake dessert of your choice. These amounts are for a 9 inch pan.

Ingredients
- 75g butter
- 200g biscuits (you can substitute any biscuit crumb here, ginger nuts or digestives work really well – ginger nuts are my favourite 😊)

Method
- Crush the biscuits until fine crumbs - you can do this in a food mixer (but mine was not happy with the hardness of the ginger nuts) or by hand, place into a bag and hit vigorously with a rolling pin (turned out to be faster and cathartic).
- Melt the butter in the microwave or in a small pan.
- Mix biscuits and butter until all the crumbs are covered,
- Put the mixture into a lined 9in flan case and press down firmly with back of a spoon
- Put into the fridge to chill for at least half an hour, longer is better

No Bake Base – Nuts & Dark Chocolate

This can be used with any no-bake dessert of your choice. These amounts are for a 9 inch pan.

Ingredients

- 180 g hazelnuts or almonds
- 2 tbsp cacao or cocoa powder
- 4 tbsp maple syrup or liquid honey
- 1 tsp pure vanilla extract
- 1/4 tsp salt

Method

No Bake Base (Nuts and Chocolate version):

- To roast nuts, preheat skillet on medium heat. Cook nuts for 4-5 minutes, stirring occasionally, until browned and fragrant. Chop roasted nuts until coarse.
- Add cacao powder, maple syrup, vanilla, salt and process or stir in a bowl until well mixed. It will smell like Nutella.
- Put the mixture into a lined 9in flan case and press down firmly with back of a spoon
- Put into the fridge to chill for at least half an hour, longer is better

Perfect Vinaigrette

This is a delicious addition to salad, or other cold platters.

Ingredients
- ¼ cup extra-virgin olive oil
- 1 ½ tablespoons white wine vinegar
- 1 teaspoon honey or maple syrup
- 1 teaspoon Dijon mustard
- Pinch of salt
- Several twists of freshly ground black pepper

Method
- To make the dressing: In a small bowl, combine all of the dressing ingredients and whisk to combine. Taste, and adjust if necessary.

Taco Seasoning

Great combination, and not just for Tacos.

Ingredients
- 2 tbsp. chilli powder
- 1 tbsp. ground cumin
- 1 1/2 tsp. smoked paprika
- 1 tsp. garlic powder
- 1 tsp. onion powder
- 1 tsp. salt
- 1 tsp. Black pepper
- 1/2 tsp. dried oregano

Method
- Mix all together and store in an airtight container.

Tikka Seasoning

Fabulous with meat or vegetables.

Ingredients
- 3 tsp Paprika
- 2 tsp Ground Coriander
- 2 tsp Ground Cumin
- 2 tsp Garam Masala
- 1.5 tsp Turmeric
- 1 tsp Ground Ginger
- 1 tsp Garlic Powder
- 1 tsp Salt
- 1/4 tsp Black Pepper
- 1/4 tsp Cayenne Pepper

Method
- Mix all of the ingredients together & place in a glass jar. Preferably one with a tight lid.

OUR LOCKDOWN COOKBOOK

The, Not in Disney Any More, Crew

USEFUL INFORMATION

Sugar to Honey Converter 180
Going Gluten Free in a Bake 181
Sourdough Starter 182
Volume & Weight Conversions 190
Temperature Conversions 191

Sugar to Honey Converter

Useful if you want to replace refined sugar in your baking with delicious honey.

Conversions

1 Tbsp Sugar=10 ml Honey

When using honey, reduce oven temperature by 25°F/15C. This will prevent over-browning.

1-3 Tbsp
- No additional baking soda needed.
- No reduction in the amount of liquid is needed.

4-6 Tbsp
- Add 1ml baking soda
- No reduction in the amount of liquid is needed.

7-12 Tbsp
- Add 2ml baking soda
- From 8 Tbsp, begin to reduce the amount of liquid needed by 20ml, increasing with each Tbsp by 2.5ml

13-15 Tbsp and 1 cup
- Add 3ml baking soda
- From 8 Tbsp, begin to reduce the amount of liquid needed by 20ml, increasing with each Tbsp by 2.5ml

Going Gluten Free in a Bake

Tips for how to remove gluten laden flour from your recipe.

Swap the flour
Substitute all-purpose gluten-free flour in place of all-purpose regular flour at a ratio of 1:1. If you are baking items such as cakes and/or breads, add 1 teaspoon of xanthan gum.

Create a gluten-free flour mixture
In place of flour in a recipe, try this combination.
- 3 parts white or brown rice flour
- 2 parts potato starch
- 1 part tapioca flour/starch
- 1 teaspoon xanthan gum for every 1-1/2 cups flour mixture

Consider arrowroot powder
Arrowroot powder can be used in place of xanthan gum if you are having a hard time finding the latter. As a rule, use 1/2 teaspoon of arrowroot powder for each cup/136g of wheat flour called for in any recipe. Note: Round up if the recipe calls for a partial cup.

Experiment with ingredients
Other ingredients in the recipe may need to be adjusted when trying new flours and flour combinations. For example, use 2-1/2 teaspoons of baking powder for every cup of flour used in a recipe. Some flours may be a bit drier, so you may have to add additional liquid ingredients, such as water or oil, depending on what the recipe calls for.

Be aware of hidden Gluten
- Some premade products may have hidden gluten, so check the ingredients (e.g. baking powder, stock cubes)

Sourdough Starter

How To Make Sourdough Starter from scratch – be patient!

Ingredients
- All-purpose flour (or a mix of all-purpose and whole grain flour)
- Water, preferably filtered

Equipment
- 2-quart glass or plastic container (not metal)
- Scale (highly recommended) or measuring cups
- Mixing spoon
- Plastic wrap or clean kitchen towel

Method
- Making sourdough starter takes about 5 days. Each day you "feed" the starter with equal amounts of fresh flour and water. As the wild yeast grows stronger, the starter will become more frothy and sour-smelling. On average, this process takes about 5 days, but it can take longer depending on the conditions in your kitchen. As long as you see bubbles and signs of yeast activity, continue feeding it regularly. If you see zero signs of bubbles after three days, take a look at the Troubleshooting section below.

Day 1: Make the Initial Starter
- 4 ounces all-purpose flour (3/4 cup plus 2 tablespoons)
- 4 ounces water (1/2 cup)
- Weigh the flour and water, and combine them in a 2-quart glass or plastic container (not metal). Stir vigorously until combined into a smooth batter. It will look like a sticky, thick dough. Scrape down the sides and loosely cover the container with plastic wrap or a clean kitchen towel secured with a rubber band.
- Place the container somewhere with a consistent room temperature of 70°F to 75°F (like the top of the refrigerator) and let sit for 24 hours.

Day 2: Feed the Starter
- 4 ounces all-purpose flour (3/4 cup + 2 tablespoons)
- 4 ounces water (1/2 cup)
- Take a look at the starter. You may see a few small bubbles here and there. This is good! The bubbles mean that wild yeast have started making themselves at home in your starter. They will eat the sugars in the the flour and release carbon dioxide (the bubbles) and alcohol. They will also increase the acidity of the mixture, which helps fend off any bad bacterias. At this point, the starter should smell fresh, mildly sweet, and yeasty.
- If you don't see any bubbles yet, don't panic — depending on the conditions in your kitchen, the average room temperature, and other factors, your starter might just be slow to get going.
- Weigh the flour and water for today, and add them to the starter. Stir vigorously until combined into a smooth batter. It will look like a sticky, thick dough. Scrape down the sides and loosely cover the container with the plastic wrap or kitchen towel secured again. Place the container somewhere with a consistent room temperature of 70°F to 75°F (like the top of the refrigerator) and let sit for 24 hours.

Day 3: Feed the Starter
- 4 ounces all-purpose flour (3/4 cup + 2 tablespoons)
- 4 ounces water (1/2 cup)
- Check your starter. By now, the surface of your starter should look dotted with bubbles and your starter should look visibly larger in volume. If you stir the starter, it will still feel thick and batter-like, but you'll hear bubbles popping. It should also start smelling a little sour and musty. Again, if your starter doesn't look quite like mine in the photo, don't worry. Give it a few more days. My starter happened to be particularly vigorous!
- Weigh the flour and water for today, and add them to the starter. Stir vigorously until combined into a smooth batter. It will look like a sticky, thick dough. Scrape down the sides and loosely cover the container with the plastic wrap or kitchen towel secured again. Place the container somewhere with a consistent room temperature of 70°F to 75°F (like the top of the refrigerator) and let sit for 24 hours.

Day 4: Feed the Starter
- 4 ounces all-purpose flour (3/4 cup + 2 tablespoons)
- 4 ounces water (1/2 cup)
- Check your starter. By now, the starter should be looking very bubbly with large and small bubbles, and it will have doubled in volume. If you stir the starter, it will feel looser than yesterday and honeycombed with bubbles. It should also be smelling quite sour and pungent. You can taste a little too! It should taste sour and somewhat vinegary.
- When I made my starter here, I didn't notice much visual change from Day 3 to Day 4, but could tell things had progress by the looseness of the starter and the sourness of the aroma.
- Weigh the flour and water for today, and add them to the starter. Stir vigorously until combined into a smooth batter. It will look like a sticky, thick dough. Scrape down the sides and loosely cover the container with the plastic wrap or kitchen towel secured again. Place the container somewhere with a consistent room temperature of 70°F to 75°F (like the top of the refrigerator) and let sit for 24 hours.

Day 5: Starter is Ready to Use
- Check your starter. It should have doubled in bulk since yesterday. By now, the starter should also be looking very bubbly — even frothy. If you stir the starter, it will feel looser than yesterday and be completely webbed with bubbles. It should also be smelling quite sour and pungent. You can taste a little too! It should taste even more sour and vinegary.
- If everything is looking, smelling, and tasting good, you can consider your starter ripe and ready to use! If your starter is lagging behind a bit, continue on with the Day 5 and Beyond instructions.

Day 5 and Beyond: Maintaining Your Starter
- 4 ounces all-purpose flour (3/4 cup + 2 tablespoons)
- 4 ounces water (1/2 cup)
- Once your starter is ripe (or even if it's not quite ripe yet), you no longer need to bulk it up. To maintain the starter, discard (or use) about half of the starter and then "feed" it with new flour and water: weigh the flour and water, and combine them in the container with the starter. Stir vigorously until combined into a smooth batter.
- If you're using the starter within the next few days, leave it out on the counter and continue discarding half and "feeding" it daily. If it will be longer before you use your starter, cover it tightly and place it in the fridge. Remember to take it out and feed it at least once a week — I also usually let the starter sit out overnight to give the yeast time to recuperate before putting it back in the fridge.

How to Reduce the Amount of Starter
- Maybe you don't need all the starter we've made here on an ongoing basis. That's fine! Discard half the starter as usual, but feed it with half the amount of flour and water. Continue until you have whatever amount of starter works for your baking habits.

How to Take a Long Break from Your Starter
- If you're taking a break from baking, but want to keep your starter, you can do two things:
- 1) Make a Thick Starter: Feed your starter double the amount of flour to make a thicker dough-like starter. This thicker batter will maintain the yeast better over long periods of inactivity in the fridge.
- 2) Dry the Starter: Smear your starter on a Silpat and let it dry. Once completely dry, break it into flakes and store it in an airtight container. Dried sourdough can be stored for months. To re-start it, dissolve 1/4 cup of the flakes in 4 ounces of water, and stir in 4 ounces of flour. Continue feeding the starter until it is active again.

# OUR LOCKDOWN COOKBOOK

Volume & Weight Conversions

Volume

US	Metric /ml
1/4 tsp	1.2
1/2 tsp	2.5
1 tsp	5
1 tbsp	15
1 fl oz	30
1/4 cup or 2 fl oz	60
1/3 cup	80
1/2 cup	120
2/3 cup	160
3/4 cup	180
1 cup, 8 fl oz	235
2 cups, 1 pint	475
4 cups, 1 quart	945
8 cups, 1/2 gall	1900
1 gallon	3800

Weight

US /oz	Metric /g	UK /oz
0.50	15	0.52
1	30	1.04
3	85	3.13
3.53	100	3.68
4	115	4.17
8	230	8.33
12	340	12.5
16, 1 lb	450	16.67

Tables contain approximate conversions for ease of use.

Exact Conversions:

US to UK oz Formula:
(US oz x 1.042) = UK oz

UK to US oz Formula:
(UK oz x 0.96) = US oz

Temperature Conversions

Gas	°F	°C	Fan Oven /°C	Jamming and Candy
	120	50		
	180	80		Fruit Bottling
	190	85		Sterilising
	212	100		Water Boiling
	220	105		Jam Set
	240	115		Soft Ball Candy
	250	120		Firm Ball Candy
	260	127		Hard Ball Candy
1	285	140	120	Soft Crack Candy
2	300	150	130	
	308	153		Hard Crack Candy
	320	160	140	
3	325	170	150	
	345	174		Caramel
4	350	180	160	
5	375	190	170	Frying Fish
6	400	200	180	Frying Chips
7	425	220	200	
8	450	230	210	
9	470	240	220	

Tables contain approximate conversions for ease of use
Exact Conversions:
Celsius to Fahrenheit Formula: (°C * 1.8) + 32 = °F
Fahrenheit to Celsius Formula: (°F - 32) / 1.8 = °C

The, Not in Disney Any More, Crew

OUR LOCKDOWN COOKBOOK

WHO SUBMITTED EACH RECIPE & WHERE IT CAME FROM

Who Shared	Recipe Title	Where
Sophie	Baked Marrow with Mushroom and Cheese Stuffing	Shared as a whole recipe
Matti	Banana, Chocolate & Rum Loaf	Shared as a whole recipe
Tasha	Banana, Oatmeal and Choc chip cookies	https://tashasthinkings.blogspot.com/2020/01/recipe-recommendation-3-ingredient.html
Sophie	Banoffee Pie (including Maple Syrup Caramel)	Shared as a whole recipe
Tasha	Best Ever Chewy Brownies	https://handletheheat.com/chewy-brownies/
Tasha	Black Bean Brownies	https://tashasthinkings.blogspot.com/2020/03/recipe-recommendation-black-bean.html
Tasha	Broccoli Casserole	https://www.eatingwell.com/recipe/256290/broccoli-casserole/
Sophie	Cheese Sauce	Shared as a whole recipe
Olwyn	Chicken Kebabs with pineapple and chilli	Shared as a whole recipe
Tasha	Chicken Tetrazzini	Preppy Kitchen https://youtu.be/EQhk7XZpZcl
Al	Chicken Tikka Kebabs	https://pinchofnom.com/recipes/chicken-tikka-kebabs/
Al	Chicken Tikka Skewers	https://pinchofnom.com/recipes/chicken-tikka-kebabs/
Tasha	Chocolate Chip Cake	https://tashasthinkings.blogspot.com/2020/05/chocolate-chip-cake-no-added-refined.html
Li	Chocolate Chunk Cookies	Shared as a whole recipe

OUR LOCKDOWN COOKBOOK

Who Shared	Recipe Title	Where
Tasha	Chocolate Date Bites	Shared as a whole recipe
Tasha	Chocolate Pudding	The Perfect Home https://youtu.be/_4bPte9X6c8
Tasha	Coconut and Mango Icecream	https://ifoodreal.com/coconut-mango-ice-cream/
Tasha	Convert to honey for baking	https://www.beemaid.com/honey-converter/
Tasha	Crumpets	https://www.redonline.co.uk/food/recipes/a501870/paul-hollywood-crumpets/
Sophie	Dates Wrapped in Bacon with Marcona Almonds	https://www.platingsandpairings.com/
Tasha	Dillegrout	Tasting History with Max Miller https://youtu.be/zk0FUS3Oq8s
Claire	Earl Grey Martini	Whittards
Beth	Egg Free Choc Chip Cookies	https://www.bbcgoodfood.com/user/4592506/recipe/egg-free-cookies
Tasha	Fridge Raid Pasta	https://tashasthinkings.blogspot.com/2020/03/recipe-fridge-raid-creamy-pasta.html
Tasha	Frying Pan Pizza	SORTEDfood https://youtu.be/B_sLZIogqGA
Tasha	Garlic & Parmesan Mash	Shared as a whole recipe
Tasha	Garlic & Parmesan Mash Waffles	Shared as a whole recipe
Sophie	General measurement conversions	Reference

Who Shared	Recipe Title	Where
Al	Glamorgan Sausages with Red Onion and Chilli Relish	https://www.bbc.co.uk/food/recipes/glamorgan_sausages_with_64911
Sophie	Gluten Free Shortbread	https://glutenfreebaking.com/how-to-make-gluten-free-shortbread/
Sophie	Going Gluten Free	https://www.tasteofhome.com/article/converting-recipes-to-gluten-free/
Olwyn	Grantham Gingers	Shared as a whole recipe
Olwyn	Grilled cheese and egg	Shared as a whole recipe
Suzy	Hash Browns	https://www.bbc.co.uk/food/recipes/hashbrowns_12454/amp
Tasha	Healthier Choc Mayo Cake with Healthy Choc Frosting	https://tashasthinkings.blogspot.com/2020/04/recipe-healthier-chocolate-mayo-cake.html
Maaike & Li	Homemade Belgian Waffles	https://thesaltymarshmallow.com/homemade-belgian-waffle-recipe/
Claire	Honey Nut Cake	https://enchantedlivingmagazine.com/hobbit-breakfast-honey-walnut-cake/
Suzy	Instant Noodles	https://thehappyfoodie.co.uk/recipes/nadiya-hussains-instant-noodles
Sophie	Italian Potato and Courgette Bake	Shared as a whole recipe
Suzy	Italian Water Cake	https://www.thepetitecook.com/water-cake/
Hazel	Jambon au Meursault	Shared as a whole recipe
Tasha	Korean Steamed Eggs	https://tashasthinkings.blogspot.com/2020/05/recipe-korean-steamed-eggs-instantpot.html
Sophie	Lamingtons	CupcakeJemma https://youtu.be/R35sgfYXdcA
Al	Lasagne	https://www.bbcgoodfood.com/recipes/classic-lasagne-0

OUR LOCKDOWN COOKBOOK

Who Shared	Recipe Title	Where
Claire	Lemon and Ginger Lemonade	Whittards
Al	Little carrot cakes with orange and honey syrup	https://www.bbcgoodfood.com/recipes/little-carrot-cakes-orange-honey-syrup
Maaike	Maaike's Pumpkin & Goats Cheese Risotto	Shared as a whole recipe
Al	Magic Custard Cake	http://www.thecooksroom.com.au/magic-custard-cake/
Claire	Mango and Bergamot G&Tea	Whittards
Beth	Mango Crumb Bars	https://www.joyousapron.com/mango-crumb-bars-4/
Sophie	Maple Chipotle Cashews	https://createmindfully.com/maple-chipotle-cashews
Sophie	Maple Syrup Caramel	Shared as a whole recipe
Sophie	Milk Bread Roll (white)	Shared as a whole recipe
Sophie	Millionaire's Shortbread with Maple Caramel	Shared as a whole recipe
Al	Miso and Honey Roast Aubergine	https://www.kikkoman.co.uk/recipes/all/miso-and-honey-roast-aubergines/
Tasha	Moist Chocolate Cake	foodCAST https://youtu.be/GgOIdkV5PPQ
Suzy	Moroccan Chicken and Lemon Soup	Shared as a whole recipe
Hazel	Mushroom Roulade	Shared as a whole recipe

The, Not in Disney Any More, Crew

Who Shared	Recipe Title	Where
Sophie	Nadia's Onion Pretzels	BBC https://youtu.be/mY9iHkEDPbw
Tasha	Nigella's Old Fashioned Sandwich Loaf	https://www.nigella.com/recipes/old-fashioned-sandwich-loaf
Tasha	No Bake Strawberry Cheesecake (Healthier)	https://ifoodreal.com/no-bake-strawberry-cheesecake/
Beth, Hazel	No Knead Crusty Chewy Bread	https://www.kingarthurflour.com/recipes/absolutely-no-knead-crusty-chewy-bread-recipe
Sophie	No-Bake Peanut and Ginger Pie	Shared as a whole recipe
Sophie	Olive and Gruyere Puff Pastry Tartlets	https://www.thelifejolie.com/olive-gruyere-puff-pastry/
Tasha	Oven Egg Bites - similar to above	https://www.flavcity.com/keto-breakfast-egg-bites/
Sophie	Patatas Bravas	http://allrecipes.co.uk/recipe/8143/patatas-bravas.aspx
Sophie	Peanut Butter and Chocolate Stuffed Cookies	Shared as a whole recipe
Suzy	Peanut Butter Brownie Baked Oatmeal	https://www.budgetbytes.com/peanut-butter-brownie-baked-oatmeal/
Tasha	Peanut Butter Swirl Brownies	Shared as a whole recipe
Beth	Perfect Cheese Scones	https://www.theguardian.com/lifeandstyle/wordofmouth/2016/oct/06/how-to-make-the-perfect-cheese-scones
Tasha	Perfect Honey & Mustard Sauce	Shared as a whole recipe
Tasha	Perfect Vinaigrette	https://cookieandkate.com/pear-date-walnut-salad-recipe/

OUR LOCKDOWN COOKBOOK

Who Shared	Recipe Title	Where
Hazel	Plum Upside Down Yoghurt Cake	https://thecafesucrefarine.com/upside-down-plum-cake/
Al	Potato & Cheese Soup	Shared as a whole recipe
Hazel	Potato Peel Soup	https://www.delicious.com.au/recipes/potato-peel-soup/
Tasha	Pumpkin Zeppole	Food Wishes https://youtu.be/-tg4iepgqSY
Al	Roasted Aubergine with Pomegranate Molasses, Feta and Mint	https://www.healthyseasonalrecipes.com/roasted-eggplant-with-pomegranate-molasses-feta-and-mint/
Hazel	Roasted Cauliflower Soup	https://cookieandkate.com/creamy-roasted-cauliflower-soup-recipe/
Sophie	Rose Sangria	https://www.bbcgoodfood.com/recipes/rose-sangria
Tasha	Rosemary & Parmessan Potato Waffles	https://tashasthinkings.blogspot.com/2020/04/recipe-rosemary-and-parmesan-potato.html
Sophie	Rosemary and Cayenne Pepper Mini Naans	Shared as a whole recipe
Sophie	Rosemary and Parmesan Oatmeal Biscuits	Shared as a whole recipe
Beth	Slow Cooker Balsamic Chicken	https://www.foodiecrush.com/slow-cooker-balsamic-chicken/
Tasha	Soft Creamy Egg Bites	https://tashasthinkings.blogspot.com/2020/04/recipe-soft-creamy-egg-bites-instantpot.html
Hazel	Soft Dinner Rolls	https://cafedelites.com/easy-soft-dinner-rolls/
Hazel	Souffle Omelette	Shared as a whole recipe

The, Not in Disney Any More, Crew

Who Shared	Recipe Title	Where
Suzy	Sourdough	https://www.thekitchn.com/how-to-make-sourdough-bread-224367
Li	Sourdough pancakes	http://supperinthesuburbs.com/2019/07/21/sourdough-pancakes
Suzy	Sourdough starter	https://www.thekitchn.com/how-to-make-your-own-sourdough-starter-cooking-lessons-from-the-kitchn-47337
Tasha	Spanish Garlic Noodles	Spain on a Fork https://youtu.be/5f2-Ph0rGsE
Tasha	Sticky Ginger Cake	https://tashasthinkings.blogspot.com/2017/08/delicious-sticky-ginger-cake.html
Maaike	Sugarfree Oatmeal Cookies	Shared as a whole recipe
Hazel	Summer Berries Drizzle Cake	https://www.bbcgoodfood.com/recipes/summer-fruit-drizzle-cake
Claire	Syrupy Lemon, Olive Oil and Semolina Cakes	https://domesticgothess.com/blog/2016/07/15/syrupy-lemon-olive-oil-semolina-cakes/
Hazel	Taco Mince Cheesy Pancakes	Shared as a whole recipe
Tasha	Taco Seasoning	https://www.delish.com/uk/cooking/recipes/a28826363/homemade-taco-seasoning-recipe/
Tasha	Tangzhong Milk Bread	https://tashasthinkings.blogspot.com/2020/06/recipe-tangzhong-milk-bread-delicious.html
Al	Teri's Cracker Barrel's Hash Brown Casserole	Shared as a while recipe
Tasha	The Best Banana Cake I've Ever Had	https://sallysbakingaddiction.com/best-banana-cake/

Who Shared	Recipe Title	Where
Beth	The Best Oatmeal Chocolate Chip Cookies	https://anitalianinmykitchen.com/chocolate-chip-cookies/
Al	Tikka Seasoning	https://pinchofnom.com/recipes/chicken-tikka-kebabs/
?	Todd's Wonder Banana Bread	Todd VanderHayden
Tasha	Tofu & Spam Fritters with Egg Fried Rice	https://tashasthinkings.blogspot.com/2020/05/recipe-tofu-spam-fritters-with-egg.html
Beth	Turkey Meatloaf	https://pinchandswirl.com/turkey-meatloaf/
Maaike	Vietnamese Breakfast Pastry (Banh Pateso)	http://atasteofjoyandlove.com/vietnamese-breakfast-pastry/
Sophie	Welsh Rarebit	Atomic Shrimp https://youtu.be/ETbq4HefLLg

LIST OF RECIPES

Breakfasts, Snacks & Soups 3

- Hash Browns 5
- Peanut Butter Brownie Baked Oatmeal 6
- Vietnamese Breakfast Pastry (Banh Pateso) (M) 8
- Moroccan Chicken and Lemon Soup (M) 10
- Potato Peel Soup 12
- Roasted Cauliflower Soup 14
- Potato & Cheese Soup 16
- Dates Wrapped in Bacon with Marcona Almonds (M) 17
- Grilled Cheese and Egg Sandwich 18
- Maple Chipotle Cashews 19
- Olive and Gruyere Puff Pastry Tartlets 20
- Patatas Bravas 21
- Welsh Rarebit 22

Main Courses & Sides 25

- Broccoli Casserole 26
- Chicken or Haloumi Kebabs with Pineapple and Chilli 28
- Chicken or Quorn Tikka Kebabs 29
- Chicken (or not) Tetrazzini 30
- Dillegrout (M) 32
- Fridge Raid Pasta 34
- Frying Pan Pizza 36
- Glamorgan Sausages with Red Onion and Chilli Relish 38
- Instant Noodles 40
- Jambon au Meursault (M) 42
- Lasagne 44
- Pumpkin & Goats Cheese Risotto 46
- Miso and Honey Roast Aubergine 47
- Mushroom Roulade 48
- Perfect Honey & Mustard Sauce + ... 50
- Roasted Aubergine with Pomegranate Molasses and Feta 51
- Slow Cooker Balsamic Chicken 52

Souffle Omelette 54
  Teri's Cracker Barrel's Hash Brown Casserole 55
  Taco Mince Cheesy Pancakes 56
  Tofu & Spam Fritters with Egg Fried Rice (M) 58
  Turkey Meatloaf (M) 60
  Baked Marrow with Mushroom and Cheese Stuffing 61
  Garlic & Parmesan Mash 62
  Garlic & Parmesan Mash Waffles 64
  Italian Potato and Courgette Bake 66
  Oven Egg Bites 67
  Korean Steamed Eggs 68
  Soft Creamy Egg Bites (Instant Pot/ Pressure cooker) 70
  Rosemary & Parmesan Potato Waffles 72
  Spanish Garlic Noodles 74

Desserts & Sweet Treats 77
  Banoffee Pie Using Maple Syrup Caramel 78
  Chocolate Date Bites 79
  Chocolate Pudding 80
  Coconut and Mango Ice Cream 81
  Gluten-Free Shortbread 82
  Homemade Belgian Waffles 83
  Millionaire's Shortbread with Maple Caramel 84
  No Bake Strawberry Cheesecake (A Healthier Option) 86
  No-Bake Peanut and Ginger Pie 88
  Sourdough Pancakes 89

Bakes 91
  Banana, Chocolate & Rum Loaf 92
  The Best Banana Cake I've Ever Had 94
  Todd's Wonder Banana Bread 96
  Banana, Oatmeal and Choc Chip Cookies 97
  Best Ever Chewy Brownies 98
  Black Bean Brownies 100
  Chocolate Chip Cake 102
  Chocolate Chunk Cookies 103
  Egg Free Choc Chip Cookies 104
  Grantham Gingers 106
  Healthier Choc Mayo Cake with Healthy Choc Frosting 108
  Honey Nut Cake 110

Italian Water Cake 112
Lamingtons 114
Little Carrot Cakes with Orange and Honey Syrup 116
Magic Custard Cake 118
Mango Crumb Bars 120
Moist Chocolate Cake 122
Peanut Butter and Chocolate Stuffed Cookies 124
Peanut Butter Swirl Brownies 126
Perfect Cheese Scones 128
Plum Upside-Down Yoghurt Cake 130
Pumpkin Zeppole 132
Rosemary and Parmesan Oatmeal Biscuits 134
Sugarfree Oatmeal Cookies 135
The Best Oatmeal Chocolate Chip Cookies 136
Summer Berries Drizzle Cake 137
Sticky Ginger Cake 138
Syrupy Lemon, Olive Oil and Semolina Cakes 140

Bread 143

Crumpets 144
Milk Bread Roll (white) 146
Nadiya's Onion Pretzels 148
Nigella's Old Fashioned Sandwich Loaf 150
No Knead Crusty Chewy Bread 152
Rosemary and Cayenne Pepper Mini Naans 154
Soft Dinner Rolls 156
Sourdough 158
Tangzhong Milk Bread 160

Cocktails 163

Earl Grey Martini 164
Lemon and Ginger Lemonade 165
Mango and Bergamot G&Tea 166
Rosé Sangria 167

Staples 169

Cheese Sauce 170
Maple Syrup Caramel 171
No Bake Base – Biscuit 172
No Bake Base – Nuts & Dark Chocolate 173

Perfect Vinaigrette	174
Taco Seasoning	175
Tikka Seasoning	176

Useful Information 179

Sugar to Honey Converter	180
Going Gluten Free in a Bake	181
Sourdough Starter	182
Volume & Weight Conversions	190
Temperature Conversions	191

Who Submitted Each Recipe & Where It Came From 193
List of Recipes 203
Index of Ingredients 207

INDEX OF INGREDIENTS

allspice, 10, 11
almonds, 17, 32, 33, 173
apple
    apple sauce, 100
arrowroot powder, 181
aubergine, 47, 51
bacon, 5, 12, 13, 17, 18, 65, 67, 70, 71
    Bacon Bits, 18
baking powder, 6, 7, 64, 65, 72, 73, 82, 83, 89, 94, 95, 100, 104, 105, 108, 109, 110, 111, 112, 113, 114, 115, 120, 121, 122, 123, 124, 126, 127, 128, 129, 130, 131, 132, 133, 134, 140, 141, 154, 181
baking soda, 89, 94, 95, 96, 98, 99, 101, 102, 108, 109, 110, 111, 122, 123, 136, 138, 180
baking spread, 138
balsamic vinegar, 40, 52, 53
banana, 6, 7, 78, 88, 92, 93, 94, 95, 96, 97, 100, 135
bay leaf, 12, 13, 52, 53
beef mince, 44, 45, 56
beef mince (lean), 44, 45
beef stock, 44, 45
beer, 22, 23
bicarbonate of soda, 92, 103, 116, 144, 145, 148
biscuits, 172
black beans, 100
black treacle, 138
blue cheese, 170
bread, 16, 18, 22, 23, 26, 27, 59, 96, 143, 146, 151, 152, 153, 158, 159, 160, 161
    breadcrumbs, 27, 38, 39, 59, 61, 62, 63, 85
broccoli, 26, 27, 59
brown sugar, 98

butter, 12, 13, 14, 15, 16, 18, 22, 23, 26, 27, 30, 31, 37, 38, 39, 42, 43, 48, 49, 52, 53, 55, 62, 63, 64, 65, 72, 73, 82, 83, 84, 85, 89, 92, 93, 94, 95, 96, 98, 99, 102, 103, 104, 105, 106, 107, 109, 110, 111, 114, 115, 118, 119, 120, 121, 122, 123, 124, 125,128, 129, 130, 134, 136, 137, 138, 145, 146, 148, 149, 150, 151, 156, 157, 160, 161, 170, 171, 172
buttermilk, 94, 95
Caerphilly, 38
carrot, 8, 10, 11, 116, 117
cashews, 19
cauliflower, 14, 15
celery, 10, 11
cheddar, 38, 55, 56, 70, 128, 170
cheese, 16, 18, 20, 22, 23, 26, 27, 30, 31, 33, 34, 35, 36, 37, 38, 39, 42, 43, 46, 48, 49, 56, 57, 61, 67, 70, 71, 75, 87, 95, 128, 129, 132, 170
cheese sauce, 56
chicken, 10, 11, 26, 28, 29, 30, 31, 32, 34, 52, 53, 55
    chicken stock, 10, 12, 26, 30, 52, 53
chicken stock, 68
chilli
    chilli flakes, 28
    chilli paste, 40, 41
    chilli powder, 21, 66, 175
    red chilli, 38
chipotle
    chipotle powder, 19
chives, 14, 15, 22, 23, 128, 129, 148, 149
chocolate, 92
    chocolate chunks, 103
    dark chocolate, 78, 79, 80, 84, 88, 100, 102, 108, 126, 127

dark chocolate chips, 97, 124
milk chocolate chips, 104
semisweet chocolate chips, 98
semisweet mini chocolate chips, 136
cinnamon, 6, 7, 83, 94, 95, 96, 107, 110, 111, 130, 132, 133, 135, 138, 139
clove, 32, 33, 47
cocoa powder, 6, 7, 79, 80, 98, 99, 100, 104, 108, 112, 113, 114, 115, 122, 124, 173
coconut milk, 81
coconut oil, 126
coffee, 100, 101, 108, 109
condensed milk, 171
Cooking Spray
   Low Calorie Cooking Spray, 29
coriander, 10, 11
   ground coriander, 176
cornmeal, 152, 153
cottage cheese, 67, 70
cream, 26, 27, 30, 31, 34, 35, 48, 49, 55, 73, 78, 80, 82, 86, 87, 88, 95, 110, 124, 125, 130, 131, 151
cream cheese, 26, 34, 67, 86, 94
creme fraiche, 48
cumin
   ground cumin, 10, 175, 176
curry powder, 10, 11
dates, 17, 79, 100, 101
desiccated coconut, 114
digestives, 172
dried herbs, 16
earl grey teabag, 164
edible flowers, 116, 117
egg, 5, 6, 7, 8, 9, 18, 20, 22, 23, 38, 39, 48, 49, 54, 58, 59, 60, 64, 65, 67, 68, 69, 70, 71, 72, 73, 83, 89, 92, 93, 94, 95, 96, 98, 99, 100, 101, 102, 103, 106, 107, 108, 109, 110, 111, 112, 114, 115, 116, 117, 118, 119, 120, 121, 122, 123, 124, 125, 126,127, 128, 129, 130, 131, 132, 135, 136, 137, 138, 139, 140, 141, 146, 147, 148, 149, 160, 161, 164, 198
Emmental, 170
feta, 51
flour, 23, 27, 31, 37, 43, 59, 66, 82, 83, 85, 89, 93, 95, 96, 98, 99, 102, 103, 105, 106, 107, 109, 110, 111, 113, 115, 117, 119, 120, 121, 122, 123, 126, 127, 129, 133, 134, 135, 136, 137, 139, 141, 143, 144, 146, 149, 151, 153, 156, 157, 158, 159, 160, 161, 170, 181, 183, 184, 185, 186, 187, 188
all purpose flour, 30, 83, 102, 108, 112
all-purpose flour, 26, 94, 98, 130, 131, 132, 158, 182, 183, 184, 185, 186, 187
bread flour, 148, 156, 158
corn flour, 50, 64, 65, 80, 82, 102, 120, 121
cornflour, 72, 73
Flour (Strong or 00), 36
plain flour, 22, 42, 58, 84, 114, 118, 124, 128, 134, 140, 170
plain white flour, 144
self-raising (rising) flour, 138
self-raising flour, 92, 104, 106, 116, 124, 128, 135, 137
strong white bread flour, 144, 146, 150, 154
Strong White Bread Flour, 160
sweet rice flour, 82
unbleached bread flour, 152
fruit, 137
gammon, 42, 43
garam masala, 176
garlic, 16, 62, 64, 74
   bulb of garlic, 74
   bulbs of garlic, 40
   crushed garlic, 34, 48, 49
   garlic clove, 14, 21, 26, 62
   garlic cloves, 10, 30, 38, 52, 63
   garlic powder, 8, 175, 176
gelatine, 86, 87
gin, 164, 165, 166
ginger
   dried ginger, 32, 33
   ground ginger, 32, 33, 106, 138, 176
   root ginger, 47
ginger nuts, 88, 172
goats cheese, 46
golden syrup, 138
gouda, 170
gruyere, 16, 20, 61, 67
haloumi, 28
ham, 34, 35, 42, 43, 70, 71
hash brown, 5, 55

Hash Brown, 5
hazelnuts, 173
herbs, 16, 49, 70, 71
honey, 10, 11, 47, 50, 81, 86, 96, 108, 109, 110, 111, 116, 117, 140, 141, 165, 173, 174, 180
ice, 166
Italian hard cheese, 30, 48
Italian herb, 34, 35
Italian seasoning, 60, 66
Italian Seasoning, 61
lasagne sheets, 44, 45
leek, 10, 11, 38, 39
lemon, 10, 11, 15, 29, 34, 35, 49, 107, 137, 140, 141, 165
    lemon juice, 14, 15, 29, 48, 49, 141, 164, 165
lemon and ginger teabag, 165
lime, 17, 137
linguine, 30
liver pate, 8
mace, 32, 33
manchego, 74
mango, 81, 120, 121
Mango and Bergamot teabag, 166
maple syrup, 19, 72, 78, 79, 81, 84, 86, 87, 92, 93, 102, 108, 126, 127, 146, 154, 155, 171, 173, 174
marrow, 61
mascarpone, 116, 117
mature cheddar, 22, 26
mayonnaise, 108
milk, 6, 7, 12, 13, 31, 33, 34, 35, 42, 43, 57, 64, 65, 70, 71, 72, 73, 80, 81, 83, 84, 88, 89, 106, 110, 111, 114, 115, 118, 119, 122, 123, 128, 129, 130, 131, 138, 139, 140, 141, 144, 146, 150, 151, 154, 155, 156, 160, 161, 170, 171
    milk powder, 160, 161
mint, 51, 167
mixed spice, 116, 117
mozzarella, 30, 31, 44, 45
mushroom, 30, 31, 48, 49, 52, 53, 60, 61
    Mushroom Ketchup, 48
mustard, 22
    Dijon, 50, 174
    English mustard, 38, 128
    English Mustard, 50
    whole grain mustard, 50

nectarine, 167
noodles, 40, 41, 74, 75
nutmeg, 14, 15, 44, 45, 96, 132, 133, 154, 170
nuts, 92, 96, 173
oatmeal, 135
oats, 6, 7, 60, 79, 97, 134, 136
oil, 5, 8, 13, 14, 16, 21, 27, 34, 35, 37, 39, 41, 45, 46, 47, 49, 50, 51, 53, 54, 56, 57, 58, 59, 61, 66, 75, 83, 85, 89, 99, 100, 113, 117, 122, 123, 127, 130, 131, 132, 133, 135, 140, 141, 145, 146, 151, 153, 154, 155, 157, 160, 161, 181
    extra virgin olive oil, 10, 14, 26, 36, 51, 52, 66, 74, 112, 140, 174
    olive oil, 44, 46, 48
    rapeseed oil, 12
    sunflower oil, 10, 12, 38, 116, 135, 140, 144
    toasted sesame oil, 47, 68
    vegetable oil, 40, 83, 98, 112, 150
olive, 20
onion, 5, 8, 10, 11, 12, 13, 14, 15, 16, 18, 21, 22, 26, 27, 30, 31, 38, 39, 40, 41, 46, 47, 50, 52, 53, 55, 56, 57, 59, 60, 64, 65, 66, 69, 148, 149
    green onion, 14, 70
    onion granules, 66, 148, 149
    onion powder, 175
    red onion, 14, 38
    shallot, 48, 49, 57
    spring onion, 18
    spring onions, 47, 58
orange, 116, 137, 167
    orange zest, 116, 117, 118
orange liqueur, 167
oregano, 48, 175
oyster sauce, 8
pancakes, 56, 57, 89
    crepes, 56
panko breadcrumbs, 58, 61
paprika, 21, 22, 23, 51, 75, 148, 149, 175, 176
    smoked paprika, 51
    Spanish paprika, 21
    sweet smoked paprika, 74
parmesan, 30, 31, 42, 48, 49, 61, 62, 63, 64, 65, 72, 73, 134, 170

parsley, 12, 13, 14, 15, 30, 31, 38, 39, 52, 53, 60, 74, 75
pea, 8, 16
  green split peas, 16
  red split peas, 16
peach, 167
peanut butter, 6, 7, 88, 124, 126
  Peanut Butter Chips, 124
  peanut butter powder, 104
pepper, 5, 13, 21, 27, 30, 31, 35, 39, 43, 48, 49, 50, 51, 53, 54, 55, 58, 60, 62, 67, 68, 69, 70, 72, 73, 75, 170
  black pepper, 8, 10, 12, 21, 38, 52, 58, 67, 174, 175, 176
  cayenne pepper, 154, 176
  ground pepper, 26, 51
  white pepper, 170
  white Pepper, 42
pine nuts, 32, 33, 46
pineapple, 28
plums, 130, 131
pomegranate molasses, 51
pomegranate seeds, 52, 53
pork, 8
potato, 5, 12, 16, 21, 33, 43, 53, 62, 63, 66
  mashed potato, 72
  potato peelings, 12, 13
potato starch, 80, 181
prosciutto, 44, 45
puff pastry, 8, 9, 20
pumpkin, 46, 132, 133
quorn, 29, 34
raisins, 10, 11, 135
red leicester, 128
rice
  long grain rice, 10
  risotto rice, 46
  white rice, 58, 82
ricotta, 34, 70, 132, 133
rose water, 32
rosemary, 50, 52, 53, 72, 73, 134, 154
rum, 92
saffron, 74, 75
sage, 12, 13
salt, 5, 6, 7, 8, 10, 11, 12, 13, 14, 15, 19, 21, 26, 27, 30, 31, 32, 33, 34, 35, 36, 37, 38, 39, 42, 43, 48, 49, 50, 51, 52, 53, 54, 55, 58, 60, 62, 63, 67, 68, 69, 70, 72, 73, 75, 82, 83, 84, 88, 94, 95, 96, 98, 99, 100, 101, 102, 108, 109, 110, 111, 113, 114, 115, 118, 119, 120, 121, 122, 123, 124, 126, 127, 128, 129, 130, 131, 132, 133, 134, 135, 136, 144, 145, 146, 148, 149, 150, 151, 152, 154, 156, 158, 160, 161, 170, 171, 173, 174, 175, 176
sausage, 39, 70, 107, 149
semolina, 36, 37, 140, 141, 152, 153
sesame seeds, 47
sour cream, 55, 150
sourdough starter, 89, 158, 183
soy sauce, 22, 23, 26, 40, 41, 47, 59, 68
spaghetti, 30, 74
Spam, 58
Spanish Noodles, 74
stock, 46
strawberries, 86, 87, 167
sugar, 6, 7, 8, 16, 32, 33, 36, 37, 39, 41, 53, 80, 82, 83, 84, 85, 89, 93, 94, 95, 96, 98, 99, 100, 102, 104, 105, 107, 110, 111, 112, 113, 115, 117, 118, 119, 120, 121, 122, 123, 125, 127, 130, 131, 133, 136, 137, 139, 140, 141, 144, 149, 151, 156, 160, 161, 164, 166, 180
  brown sugar, 40, 52, 94, 96, 103, 120, 126, 136
  caster sugar, 92, 103, 106, 114, 118, 124, 140, 144, 148, 150, 154
  dark brown sugar, 138
  golden caster sugar, 137, 167
  icing sugar, 94, 95, 114, 116, 118
  light brown muscovado sugar, 38
  light brown sugar, 98, 124, 130
  light muscovado sugar, 116
  powdered sugar, 122
  white sugar, 132
sugar syrup, 164
taco seasoning, 56, 175
thyme, 38, 39, 48
tikka
  Tikka Seasoning, 29, 176
tofu, 34, 58, 59
tomato, 21, 57
  ketchup, 49, 60, 71
  tomato paste, 52, 53
  tomato puree, 42, 43
  tomato sauce, 36, 37, 44, 45

tonic water, 166
turkey, 60
turmeric, 176
vanilla, 6, 7, 82, 83, 86, 87, 88, 89, 94, 95, 98, 99, 100, 101, 102, 104, 105, 108, 109, 112, 113, 114, 115, 118, 119, 120, 121, 122, 123, 124, 126, 127, 130, 131, 132, 133, 137, 173
vegetable stock, 12, 14, 16, 26, 30, 31, 68, 74, 75
vegetarian mince, 44, 56
walnuts, 79, 110, 111
water, 8, 9, 20, 21, 27, 31, 33, 35, 36, 37, 41, 47, 50, 56, 57, 58, 63, 67, 68, 69, 71, 81, 86, 87, 104, 105, 108, 109, 112, 113, 122, 123, 128, 129, 134, 141, 144, 145, 146, 147, 148, 149, 150, 151, 152, 156, 158, 160, 165, 166, 167, 181, 182, 183, 184, 185, 186, 187, 188, 191

white lasagne sauce, 44
white miso paste, 47
wine
  dry white wine, 42
  red wine, 21
  Spanish rosé wine, 167
  sweet white wine, 32
  white wine, 21, 32, 38, 43, 48
  wine vinegar, 21, 32, 38, 174
Worcestershire sauce, 22, 23, 26, 27
Worcestershire Sauce, 48
xanthan gum, 82, 181
yeast, 36, 37, 143, 144, 146, 148, 149, 150, 151, 152, 154, 156, 160, 161, 183, 184, 187, 188
yoghurt, 29
  greek yoghurt, 86, 130
  Greek yoghurt, 10, 108
  natural yoghurt, 116

Printed in Great Britain
by Amazon